THE
UNEXPECTED
ADVENTURE

Resources by Lee Strobel

The Case for the Real Jesus

Finding the Real Jesus

The Case for Christ

The Case for Christ — Student Edition (with Jane Vogel)

The Case for Christ for Kids (with Rob Suggs)

The Case for Christmas

The Case for a Creator

The Case for a Creator — Student Edition (with Jane Vogel)

The Case for a Creator for Kids (with Rob Suggs)

The Case for Easter

The Case for Faith

The Case for Faith — Student Edition (with Jane Vogel)

The Case for Faith for Kids (with Rob Suggs)

Faith Under Fire (curriculum series)

God's Outrageous Claims

Inside the Mind of Unchurched Harry and Mary

Off My Case for Kids (with Robert Elmer)

Surviving a Spiritual Mismatch in Marriage (with Leslie Strobel)

Resources by Mark Mittelberg

Becoming a Contagious Christian (with Bill Hybels)

Becoming a Contagious Christian Training Course,
updated DVD edition (with Lee Strobel and Bill Hybels)

Becoming a Contagious Church, updated edition

The Journey: A Bible for the Spiritually Curious
(with Judson Poling, et al., eds.)

Choosing Your Faith ... In a World of Spiritual Options

Choosing Your Faith New Testament

THE UNEXPECTED ADVENTURE

TAKING EVERYDAY RISKS TO TALK WITH PEOPLE ABOUT JESUS

LEE STROBEL
MARK MITTELBERG

Bestselling Authors

 ZONDERVAN®

 WILLOW
Willow Creek Resources

ZONDERVAN.com/
AUTHORTRACKER
follow your favorite authors

ZONDERVAN

The Unexpected Adventure
Copyright © 2009 by Lee Strobel and Mark Mittelberg

This title is also available as a Zondervan ebook. Visit www.zondervan.com/ebooks.

This title is also available in a Zondervan audio edition. Visit www.zondervan.fm.

Requests for information should be addressed to:

Zondervan, *Grand Rapids, Michigan 49530*

Library of Congress Cataloging-in-Publication Data

Strobel, Lee, 1952–
        The unexpected adventure : taking everyday risks to talk with people about
Jesus / Lee Strobel and Mark Mittelberg.
            p.   cm.
        Includes bibliographical references (p. 287).
        ISBN 978-0-310-28392-8 (softcover)
        1. Evangelistic work. I. Mittelberg, Mark. II. Title.
BV3790.S887   2009
248'.5—dc22   2008051817

Interior design by Beth Shagene

Printed in the United States of America

---

10 11 12 13 14 • 23 22 21 20 19 18 17 16 15 14 13 12 11 10 9 8 7 6 5 4

TABLE OF CONTENTS

WHEN ETERNITY HOLDS ITS BREATH

LEE STROBEL

It was a hectic day at the newspaper where I worked as an editor. Several major stories erupted before deadline. Reporters were scurrying around as they frantically tried to finish their articles. With emotions frayed, just about everyone lost their tempers.

On many days, the stress of journalism caused me to lose my composure too. But as a fairly new Christian, I asked God for his help as soon as the day looked like it was going to spiral out of control. Thanks to him, I managed to stay uncharacteristically calm amidst the chaos.

After the last story was edited, I looked up and was surprised to see one of my bosses standing over my desk. *Uh-oh!* That wasn't a good sign. But it turned out that he wasn't there to upbraid me about some mistake or oversight. Instead, he took me off guard by asking with genuine curiosity, "Strobel, how did you get through the day without blowing your top?"

Then, apparently suspecting a link between my behavior and the fact that I went to church on Sundays, he added the words that sent a chill down my spine: "What's this Christianity thing to you?"

Whoa! For a moment I froze. Nobody had ever asked me anything like that before. In fact, I had never shared my faith with anyone. The only way my boss even knew I attended church was because I once told him I couldn't go on an outing with him on a Sunday morning. And now, out of the blue, I was being put on the spot.

I didn't know what to say or how to say it. I was afraid I would utter the wrong words. I didn't want to embarrass myself or have him make fun of me. I fretted about what would happen to my career if I gushed about my faith and became known as the newsroom's "holy roller." There was a lot at stake.

My mind raced. Maybe I could dismiss the whole thing with a joke: *Christianity? Hey, what happens in church stays in church.* Maybe I could simply pretend I didn't hear him over the din of the newsroom: *Yeah, it was a crazy day. Man, look at the time! I've gotta get home or Leslie's gonna kill me!*

That's when the uninvited words of the apostle Paul coursed through my mind: "I am not ashamed of the gospel" (Romans 1:16). *Great,* I thought. *Just what I needed—a biblical guilt trip.*

Though it seemed as if minutes were ticking by, all of this occurred in a flash. Finally, even as I was opening my mouth to reply, I made a scary split-second decision: I resolved to take a spiritual risk.

I looked up at my boss. "You really want to know? Let's go into your office."

Behind closed doors, we talked for forty-five minutes. Well, to be honest, I did most of the talking. I was really nervous. Never having been trained in how to engage with others about my faith, I fumbled around and wasn't nearly as clear as I could have been. Still, in my own sincere but admittedly inept way, I tried to de-

> I made a scary split-second decision: I resolved to take a spiritual risk.

scribe how I met Jesus and the difference he had made in my life.

An amazing thing happened. He didn't laugh. He didn't make fun of me. He didn't nervously try to change the topic or make excuses so he could leave the room. Instead, he listened intently. By the end, he was hanging on every word.

At the same time, I felt like I was going to burst on the inside. It instantly became clear to me that nothing was as urgent or exciting as what I was doing in this seemingly serendipitous conversation. It felt as if time were standing still, as if eternity were holding its breath.

I'm not sure how God used that conversation in my boss's life, but I do know this: he undeniably used it in mine. When I emerged from that office, I was thoroughly invigorated. It felt like the air was carbonated! There are no words to adequately describe the thrill I felt in having been used by God to communicate his message of hope to someone far from him. It was as if my entire life up to that point had been a movie shot in very grainy black-and-white 16 mm film with scratchy sound — but those forty-five minutes were in vivid Technicolor with rich Dolby stereo.

I wanted more of that action! At that moment I knew I could never go back to my humdrum Christian experience, drifting aimlessly through my spiritual life on a tranquil sailboat atop waters unperturbed by wind and waves. For the first time, I understood that these unscripted adventures on the high seas of personal evangelism are what give excitement, fulfillment, and ultimate purpose to a life of faith. After all, what's more important than being a messenger for the Creator of the universe to someone whose eternity is hanging in the balance?

I had stumbled upon the unexpected adventure of talking with others about Jesus, and I quickly learned that living on this evangelistic edge amplifies every detail of the Christian life:

- It's where our Bible study becomes much more intense, because we're not merely reading Scripture as a devotional or academic exercise, but we're searching for fresh insights and wisdom to use in reaching our spiritually confused neighbors.

- It's where our prayer life becomes ever more focused, because we're pleading for God's help and guidance in bringing the gospel to family members who don't know Christ.

- It's where our worship becomes increasingly heartfelt, because we're praising the God of the second chance, who in his astonishing grace loves our wandering friends even more than we do.

- It's where our dependence on God reaches new heights, because we know that apart from the Holy Spirit there's no way we can bring anyone to the point of putting their trust in Jesus.

This is the missing ingredient in so many Christian lives. I've never heard anyone complain by saying, "My spiritual life is so dry right now; it's like I'm living in a desert," and then add, "Oh, by the way, I'm actively trying to reach a friend for Christ."

As I've traveled the world, I've repeatedly found that it's the Christians living out the unexpected adventure who are enjoying the most fulfilling relationships with God. For them, a day might start out average and routine, but it always has the potential to blossom into a life-changing and eternity-altering encounter.

I've seen this happen countless times. For instance, I invited my ministry partner, Mark Mittelberg, and another leader from our church to visit the place where I had covered some of the city's most notorious trials when I was legal editor of the *Chicago Tribune*.

As the elevator door opened on the twenty-first floor in the federal courthouse, I immediately recognized a figure standing in the hallway: he was a competitor of mine from another news organization back in the days when I was a wild-living, hard-drinking atheist. He was one of those tough Chicago reporters, with a big, unlit stogie that he just gnawed all day.

"Strobel!" he snarled when he saw me. "How the [blank] are you? I haven't seen you in years! Are you still writing for that [blankety-blank] *Chicago Tribune*, that [blankety-blank] piece of [blankety-blankety-blank]?"

"Actually, I've had a big change in my life," I told him. "I've become a Christian — and I'm a pastor now."

His cigar almost fell out of his mouth. In his amazement, all he could mutter was: "I'll be damned!"

"Well," I replied, "you don't *have* to be." And with that, God gave me an opportunity to talk with him a bit about Jesus!

I could never have foreseen that happening. The day had started out mundane and ordinary, but suddenly I was presented with an opportunity to talk about critically important eternal issues with someone I hadn't seen in almost a decade. *This is the unexpected adventure!*

Look at Jesus: he lived out the unexpected adventure throughout his ministry. People were constantly walking up to him out of nowhere and abruptly raising spiritual questions, such as the rich young ruler who suddenly appeared and asked, "What must I do to be saved?" Admittedly, that was more refined than "I'll be damned," but it was unexpected just the same (at least to the disciples).

And how did Jesus handle this overachiever? He enthusiastically entered into the adventure, lovingly challenging him to give up everything keeping him from God so that he could get in on the adventure himself.

Paul did the same thing. As he moved from place to place, he created action — and often controversy — wherever he went. One person summed up Paul's impact by saying he sparked revivals or riots wherever he would speak. In other words, his life was one big moving adventure.

In fact, Paul summed up the kind of life we can all live by saying we should be ready to communicate God's message "in season and out of season" (2 Timothy 4:2). In effect, he was saying, "Be ready for the adventure of sharing your faith when it's expected and when it's unexpected!" Eugene Peterson put it this way in *Traveling Light*:

> The word "Christian" means different things to different people. To one person it means a stiff, upright, inflexible way of life, colorless and unbending. To another, it means a risky, surprise-filled venture, lived tiptoe at the edge of expectation.... If we get our information from the biblical material, there is no doubt that the Christian life is a dancing, leaping, daring life.[1]

At the edge of expectation — that's how we're meant to live life. When we tell God, "Please surprise me with opportunities to tell others about you," we can have confidence that he will take us on white-knuckle adventures that will make an eternal impact on others while at the same time giving us the thrills of a lifetime. It's the difference between a numb life of predictability and an exhilarating series of divine "coincidences."

What kind of coincidences? Well, one average and routine day I was packing up my briefcase and getting ready to leave the newspaper when I felt a gentle nudging of the Holy Spirit. I sensed God wanted me to go into the business office and invite my friend, who was an atheist, to come to Easter services at my church. Since the impression seemed so strong, I figured something dramatic was going to happen. And it did — but not in the way I had anticipated.

I walked into the business office and looked around. The place appeared empty except for my friend, who was sitting at his desk. *Perfect!* I reminded him that Easter was coming and asked if he would want to come to church with Leslie and me. He turned me down cold. I asked if he was interested at all in spiritual matters, and he emphatically said no. I asked if he had any questions about God, and again he said no. I talked to him about why the resurrection was so important, but he clearly wasn't interested.

With all of my evangelistic overtures being instantly shut down, I was beginning to get a little embarrassed. Why was he so disinterested in talking about spiritual matters if God was indeed prodding me to talk with him? Finally, I stammered, "Well, uh, if you've ever got any questions, um, I guess you know where my desk is," and I walked out.

What was that all about? I couldn't understand why he was so adamantly resistant. In the end, I concluded that maybe I was going to be one link in a very long chain of people and experiences that would eventually lead him to Christ. Still, as far as I know he remains a skeptic to this day.

Fast-forward several years. By this time I was a teaching pastor at Willow Creek Community Church in suburban Chicago. After I spoke one Sunday morning, a middle-aged man came up, shook my hand, and said, "I just want to thank you for the spiritual influence you've had in my life."

"That's very nice," I said, "but who are you?"

"Let me tell you my story," he replied. "A few years ago I lost my job. I didn't have any money, and I was afraid I was going to lose my house. I called a friend of mine who runs a newspaper and said, 'Do you have any work for me?' He asked, 'Can you tile floors?' Well, I had tiled my bathroom once, so I said, 'Sure.' He told me, 'We need some tiling done at the newspaper. If you can do that, we can pay you.'

"So one day, not long before Easter, I was on my hands and knees behind a desk in the business office of the newspaper, fixing some tiles, when you walked into the room. I don't think you even saw me. You started talking about God and Jesus and Easter and the church to some guy, and he wasn't interested at all. But I was crouching there listening, and my heart was beating fast, and I started thinking, '*I need God!* I need to go to church!'

"As soon as you left, I called my wife and said, 'We're going to church this Easter.' She said, 'You're kidding!' I said, 'No, we are.' We ended up coming to this church that Easter, and my wife, my teenage son, and I all came to faith in Christ. I just wanted to thank you."

I was dumbstruck! Who could have foreseen that, except the amazing God of grace?

Anyone who has ever read the Bible knows that God wants us to be involved with spreading his good news far and wide. What is mysterious is why he chooses to include *us* in his redemptive mission. Could it be because of the way he uses unexpected adventures to enrich our lives?

Inevitably, our faith is deepened when we sense God leading us into evangelistic encounters, when we see him answer our prayers for spiritually befuddled friends, and when we witness how the gospel continues to revolutionize people who put their trust in Christ.

The truth is that I've become a fanatic when it comes to radical life change. Nothing is more fulfilling than seeing ordinary people turned into extraordinary followers of God, imbued with his Spirit and enabled by his power to make incredible differences in the lives of others.

Atheists who become missionaries. Once wayward kids who

are now inspired worship leaders. Hardened inmates who become compassionate pastors. Disengaged dads who turn into the enthusiastic leaders of Christ-centered families. Narcissists who become selfless servants of others. Former drug abusers who rescue the lives — and souls — of addicts. Ordinary folks who thought they had it all until they discovered there's nothing more important than Jesus. *Is there anything better?*

This is what gets me up in the morning: the thought that somehow, in some way, God might take this seemingly routine day and surprise me with an opportunity to tell someone about the good news that has the power to turn their life inside out.

Don't you want more of this action in your life? My guess is that you've got old friends from school, colleagues at work, neighbors down the block, and even members of your own family who you fear will stare into a Christless abyss after they close their eyes for the last time in this world. You know that God has the ability to redeem, restore, and redirect them, giving them new values, a fresh purpose, and renewed priorities. After all, he has a history of doing that with the most unlikely characters — including people like you and me.

The reason that Mark Mittelberg and I wrote this book is to help you start engaging in your own evangelistic episodes. For more than twenty years, Mark and I have been friends and ministry partners. Individually and together, we've repeatedly found ourselves embroiled in unexpected adventures. Sometimes we've been scared to death; other times we've been doubled over with laughter. And time after time we've shaken our heads in amazement and gratitude as we've seen God surpass all of our expectations.

But I might as well confess this up front: we've also made every outreach mistake in the book and then some. Yet despite our occasional ineptitude, even with our hesitations and failings, we've seen God energize our efforts and bring many friends and strangers several steps forward in their spiritual journeys — sometimes even all the way to the point of repentance and faith.

As you can imagine, we've learned a lot of lessons along the way, and we'll be passing them along in the following pages as we tell stories from our own adventures. Our unabashed goal is to paint a real-life picture of personal evangelism that's so compelling, so desirable, so irresistible, and so darn do-able that you will be anxious to take the next step yourself — whatever that is — in engaging in your own adventures. Maybe that step is merely to meet someone new; perhaps it's to get into a spiritual conversation; or it could be to explain the gospel and pray with someone to receive Christ.

You don't need to have all the answers to every theological question. You don't have to master a polished gospel presentation that you mechanically recite whether people want to hear it or not. You don't have to pretend you're the next Billy Graham. All you have to do is authentically follow Christ in your own life and ask him to ambush you with opportunities, then trust that he's going to use you in spite of (and sometimes even *because* of) your shortcomings, foibles, and quirks.

Simply put, our role is this: *to be ready and willing — because God is always able.* After all, *he* is the great evangelist; we're merely the tools that he uses to fulfill his mission of redeeming the world, one individual at a time.

So go ahead, read an episode a day over the next six weeks. Ask God to ignite or intensify your fire for reaching people with his message of forgiveness and eternal life. And don't forget to get a pad of paper ready. You're going to want to start compiling your own list of stories as God inevitably takes you on a series of unforgettable and unexpected adventures.

ENROLLING IN THE ADVENTURE

MARK MITTELBERG

"So, Mark, are you a Christian?"

Terry's seemingly simple question was actually quite intimidating in that era of my life. We had been friends ever since we attended middle school together. I'd always appreciated his direct personality — at least until that particular moment, when he was challenging me about the inconsistencies in my life.

"Sure, I'm a Christian, Terry. What about it?" I replied somewhat defensively while trying not to raise my voice too much. I didn't want my coworkers to overhear our conversation, fearing it would ruin my reputation and spoil some of the fun I had partying with them.

I was nineteen years old and living large — or at least I thought I was. I worked in an electronics store that sold high-end stereo equipment as well as round vinyl objects called "records," which looked like oversized CDs and played music on devices called "turntables." (If you're under thirty, you'll probably need to look up these things on the Internet or in a history book, where you'll find details and maybe a few pictures to help you understand what I'm talking about.)

Suffice it to say, we sold really good sound equipment and played great music on it — *loud*! It was an exciting place for a young guy like me to work. I enjoyed the environment, the money, the friends, and the freedom that this season of my life brought. Thoughts of God, church, and religion were low on my list of concerns.

Then on that fateful day, Terry walked into the store, eager to make a point. For whatever reason, he felt compelled to challenge my spiritual complacency.

In Columbo-like fashion, Terry responded to my claim of faith with another question: "How can you call yourself a Christian and yet do so many things that Christians don't do?"

"Well," I said flippantly, "I guess I'm just a *cool* Christian." Rarely have stupider words been spoken, but it was the best I could come up with at the time.

My remark didn't go over well with Terry. Without batting an eye, he shot back, "Oh, really? Don't you know there's a word for 'cool Christians'?"

I shook my head, though he wasn't really waiting for a reply.

"They're called *hypocrites*!" Terry spat out.

Ouch!

Not knowing quite how to handle his verbal missile, I did what came naturally — I returned fire: "Oh, yeah? So what about *your* life, Terry? Are you telling me you've got it all together?"

"No," he replied, a bit more gently. "But at least I'm honest about it."

Even after Terry left, his words lingered. I felt angry. *Who does he think he is, coming in here and talking to me like that?* It wasn't until a day or two later, after I'd cooled down, that I finally realized why his challenge bothered me so much: I knew he was right.

As I kept replaying that conversation in my mind, I felt a

gradual softening in my attitude. My initial anger was replaced with reflection — and within a few days that reflection turned into repentance.

Finally, after a combination of divinely orchestrated influences over the previous few weeks — including the prayers of my visiting grandmother Effa, the encouragement of my mom, some sobering conversations with my dad, the godly example of my siblings, the challenges of several sermons from a couple of gifted teachers, the influence of some new friends at a Bible study I had visited, and now the rebuke by Terry — I finally decided on the evening of November 8, 1976, to give up the fight and yield my life to Christ. I asked for his full and free forgiveness, and I told him I wanted to follow him from that day forward, all the way into eternity.

I've never been the same since that day. I immediately became aware of God's presence and leadership in my life, and I felt a new sense of mission. I realized that I was put on the planet not just to know God personally but also to spread his love and truth to the people around me.

I didn't quit my job, rush off to seminary, or join a ministry somewhere. Instead I looked for ways to be used right where I was. God opened the doors and began guiding me into spiritual conversations with friends, coworkers, and occasionally even customers — some of whom ended up trusting in Christ.

God also gave me opportunities to impact lives through teaching high school classes at my church, through helping lead the Bible study I had begun attending, and through efforts with some friends to bring contemporary Christian music groups to our town to play outreach-oriented concerts.

Two words describe all that I began experiencing. The first is *unexpected*. If you had told me just a week or two before that conversation with Terry that I would soon become impassioned about talking to people about faith, I would have laughed out loud. That's because I hadn't been walking with God or known the exhilaration of being used by him to touch the lives of others.

You can probably guess the second word: *adventure*. I hadn't anticipated that knowing Christ, seeking to follow his will each day, taking risks to raise spiritual topics of conversation, answering people's questions, making the gospel message clear, and seeing lives changed by God's Spirit working through me would all be so thrilling. It exceeded by a long shot any kind of excitement I'd ever experienced before. As Lee puts it, it offered "thrills that fulfill."

The kind of thrills, I might add, that every one of us is made to experience and enjoy.

⋯> Action Principle

You may not have realized it before, but as a Christian you too are called into the unexpected adventure of spreading the faith to others. How do I know? Because a "Christian," by definition, is a follower of Jesus Christ, the one who came "to seek and to save what was lost" (Luke 19:10) and who then commissioned us to follow his example and "go and make disciples" (Matthew 28:19). We were redeemed, in part, for the purpose of reaching others for Christ. Therefore, we'll never be complete in our experience with God until we allow him to use us to spread his message to others.

⋯> Stepping into the Adventure

I knew from childhood that I should follow Christ, and I had taken stabs at doing so along the way — but in later years I had resisted it. Why? In part, ironically, because I was afraid that God was going to take away my fun and sense of adventure. I had convinced myself that Christianity, though correct in its teachings, was a lifestyle for people who couldn't do much else. It certainly did not evoke in me thoughts of risk-taking or excitement.

Can you relate to that? Part of the problem, I guess, is a response to some of the religious people around us. They're nice people, but risk and adventure seem to have left their lives somewhere in the last millennium — if they were ever there in the first place. It's not surprising if we react to their examples with a yawn. Churches can be pretty sleepy places, and we need to change that.

> Begin to transform the culture of your church by first seeking God's revival in your own soul.

You can begin to transform the culture of your church by first seeking God's revival in your own soul, reinstating in your own heart his vision for reaching this lost and dying world. Cultivate passion and excitement for the unexpected adventure, and you'll be amazed at how you — regardless of your age, gender, background, or experience — can stir up your church to become a more spiritually dynamic and contagious place.

Another reason we might have misconceptions of the Christian life is because we underestimate God's character and misunderstand his desires for us. We think, strangely, that his goal is to curtail our freedom and stifle our spirit so that he can somehow better contain and control us. But this is a woefully mistaken perception of the all-powerful and all-wise God, who created beauty, nature, color, emotion, art, and life itself — not to mention ingrained in us the desire for adventure and excitement.

No, our God is the God of creativity and imagination. He's an unpredictable being of perfection as well as spontaneity. He cares for the people he created with a strong and undying love, and he wants to use each of us in surprising ways to reach others with his life-changing gospel as part of his amazing redemptive plan for the entire world.

Now *that's* adventure, and it involves *you.*

› Inspiration for the Journey

God, who got you started in this spiritual adventure, shares with us the life of his Son and our Master Jesus. He will never give up on you. Never forget that.

1 Corinthians 1:8 – 9, *The Message*

WHEN YOU JUST DON'T KNOW

LEE STROBEL

"Aw, isn't that cute?" I said to Leslie as I hung up the telephone. "This is gonna be fun."

At the time, I was a fairly new Christian serving on a team of volunteers who contacted visitors after they submitted inquiries on cards at our weekend services. One Sunday, a pleasant and precocious twelve-year-old girl submitted a question, simple and sincere: "I want to know more about Jesus." When I telephoned her, she invited Leslie and me to her apartment to talk with her and her father about Christ.

Wow, this is a great opportunity! I thought. *What could be better than this?*

Leslie and I were full of anticipation as we drove to their home the following Friday evening. As her father opened the door and we walked in, I glanced at the coffee table in the living room and saw stacks of heavyweight books. It turns out her dad was a scientist who had spent years studying scholarly articles and weighty tomes attacking the foundations of Christianity.

We sat down at the dining room table for pizza and soft drinks. Soon he was peppering me with tough objections to the reliability of the New Testament, the divinity of Jesus, and the credibility of the Old Testament. He challenged the resurrection and the Trinity. He leveled a lot of arguments against the faith that he had learned in studying the writings of atheists and other critics.

While I was able to answer some of his questions, he kept raising issues that I had never even considered. Before long my head was starting to spin. I felt what I call "spiritual vertigo," that queasy sense of dizziness and disorientation when someone challenges the core of your faith in a way that you cannot answer. My *own* faith was starting to quiver.

Have you ever felt spiritual vertigo? If you haven't, you probably will — and soon, because challenges to the biblical understanding of Jesus are mounting in best-selling books, popular magazines, college classrooms, television documentaries, and on the Internet. If you're serious about embarking on the unexpected adventure by seizing opportunities to get into spiritual conversations with friends and neighbors, then before long someone is going to level a challenge that you have no idea how to answer.

I kept munching my pizza and sipping my drink, hoping and praying for profound insights to spring into my mind. But I was blank. I wasn't going to be able to bluff my way through this. That's when I put down my glass, looked him in the eye, and said the words that instantly had a liberating effect on me.

"Frankly," I admitted, "I don't know the answers to those questions."

Rather than feeling defeated, I suddenly experienced a sense of calm. In that moment, I realized it was okay not to have the answer to every conceivable question at the tip of my tongue. Few people in the world could have extemporaneously responded to the wide-ranging challenges he was raising.

I began to look on the positive side: Here was someone with

legitimate objections who was willing to engage in a dialogue about the most important issues of life. And equally important, here was his impressionable daughter sitting by his side, wondering whether Jesus was worth believing in.

This *was* an opportunity!

In circumstances like these, "I don't know" might very well be the best response we can give. One of my friends, Cliffe Knechtle, author of *Give Me an Answer*, is an expert in dealing with tough questions about the faith. Part of his ministry involves traveling from university to university, where he spontaneously engages skeptical students and professors who have objections to Christianity. More than once, I've seen him step back from a particularly nettlesome attack and give the only appropriate reply: "I ... do ... not ... know," he says, emphasizing each word.

> "I don't know" might very well be the best response we can give.

There are times when the Bible is silent on an issue, and it's best not to hazard a reply that might not have a scriptural basis. In other instances we have a gap in our knowledge and have no idea how to respond. We don't want anyone to think we're stupid or ill-informed, and yet the honest truth is that it's better to confess ignorance than try to manufacture an explanation out of thin air.

Go ahead, say it out loud: *"I ... do ... not ... know."* Now look around. The sky isn't falling!

But it's important to note that I didn't stop there with the scientist and his daughter. "You've raised a lot of good issues," I said at the conclusion of the evening. "But I suspect that after two thousand years, you haven't come up with the objection that's finally going to topple Christianity. So let me investigate as honestly as I can and get back to you."

And sure enough, as I checked into each and every one of

his challenges, I found answers that satisfied my heart and mind — without exception. When I looked at the other side of these issues, I found facts, logic, and evidence that once again reinforced my own faith and gave me material to pass along to the scientist.

I've lost track of the girl and her father through the years, so I don't know whether either of them ever put their trust in Christ. But thanks to our conversation late into that difficult Friday evening, I became equipped to address similar objections to Christianity. The next time, instead of being seized by spiritual vertigo, I was ready.

Still, there are those times when I have to confess: "I ... do ... not ... know." And that's okay. I've learned not to be afraid of those words. I've found they can actually lead to even more exciting spiritual interaction as long as we follow them with: "But let me help you find out."

> Action Principle

When someone raises an objection to Christianity that you can't answer, the best response isn't to sputter or sulk, to get flustered or angry, or to make up an explanation just so you have something to say. Tell the person with sincerity that you simply don't know, and then invite him or her to pursue the answers with you.

> Stepping into the Adventure

When I taught First Amendment law at Roosevelt University, I stressed to budding journalists that it was vitally important for them to understand exactly where the lines are drawn in the laws against libel and invasion of privacy. The reason wasn't just so they could avoid getting hauled into court. If a reporter isn't sure what's safe to print, he naturally tends to censor himself, shrinking back from writing what he ought to be publishing because he's afraid of running afoul of the law.

In a similar way, Christians often miss the adventure of spiritual conversations because they're afraid they're going to get asked a question they can't answer. They don't feel very conversant with why they believe what they believe, and consequently they censor themselves and avoid evangelistic interactions altogether so they won't be embarrassed by what they don't know.

That's a good reason to comply with 1 Peter 3:15: "Always be prepared to give an answer to everyone who asks you to give the reason for the hope that you have." When we have done enough study to have an adequate factual foundation for our faith, we naturally become more willing to engage with people who may have doubts.

None of us, however, knows the answer to every possible question a skeptic might raise. When a seemingly unanswerable issue confronts you, remember that Christianity has withstood similar challenges for two millennia. Keep in mind that it's a good thing when an individual has questions. This could very well be an open door to further conversations as you invite him or her to check out the evidence with you.

In fact, what could have been a single interaction about Christianity can lead to an ongoing dialogue as you use books, the Internet, and other materials to help your friend find answers to his questions over time. (We have included a list of suggested materials in the back of this book.)

Why not say, "Hey, that's a tough topic. I really don't know how to respond to it. How about if I find a book we can read on

> When a seemingly unanswerable issue confronts you, remember that Christianity has withstood similar challenges for two millennia.

the issue and then we get together on Tuesday night at the coffee shop to talk about it?"

If you have several friends with similar questions, consider starting a small group in which you can pursue answers together over a period of time. My friend Garry Poole spells out how to lead these groups in his excellent book *Seeker Small Groups*.

Please, don't miss the unexpected adventure because you're nervous that you might have to utter those words "I ... do ... not ... know." After all, that *is* the adventure: delving into conversations that could go in who-knows-what direction, confident that God will guide you toward answers for yourself *and* for your friend.

> Inspiration for the Journey

My dear friends, if you know people who have wandered off from God's truth, don't write them off. Go after them. Get them back and you will have rescued precious lives from destruction and prevented an epidemic of wandering away from God.

James 5:19 – 20, *The Message*

BEING YOUR OWN ECCENTRIC SELF

MARK MITTELBERG

"Let me know if you have any questions," said the waiter as he leaned against a pillar in our out-of-the-way section of a popular restaurant.

It was an exciting but stressful time in my life. Heidi and I had recently moved from our small Midwestern hometown to the big city of Chicago so I could attend graduate school. With a background in business, I was feeling overwhelmed as I began to work on my master's degree in philosophy of religion.

It wasn't that I didn't enjoy the new subject matter or appreciate my professors. I found the studies fascinating. But have you ever tried to *read* any of Kant's *Critique of Pure Reason*? Try the opening sentence: "In whatever manner and by whatever means a mode of knowledge may relate to objects, intuition is that through which it is in immediate relation to them, and to which all thought as a means is directed."[2]

I don't know about you, but I was pretty sure I could have survived in life without ever having read that information. I was often tempted to ask the question that students frequently ponder: "Are we ever going to really *use* any of this stuff, or is this just a way to see who's fully committed to getting a degree?"

My mind was full of those kinds of thoughts that evening as Heidi and I, along with some new friends from school, sat down at this well-known Italian eatery. The aroma of freshly baked Chicago-style stuffed pizzas wafted through the air. The waiter who seated us was friendly and outgoing. It was after he had gotten us our drinks that he leaned against the pillar and posed his offer to answer any questions we might have.

The restaurant was starting to fill up, causing the rest of the waiters and waitresses to scurry around in order to handle the surge of people. So I was surprised that he was so casually lingering by our table — until I realized that we were in an area that was out of the sight of his boss. The waiter was using us as an occasion for a break. I think he was hoping we would have questions about, say, how they tossed their pizza dough or what ingredients went into their sauce. Just so he wouldn't have to move his feet for a few minutes.

What struck me was how open-ended his offer had been. He had simply invited us to tell him if we had any questions — but he hadn't specified that they needed to be related to the menu. An idea hit me, and it came with enough force that I wondered if the Holy Spirit might be prompting it: *I've got all kinds of questions. Maybe I'll put what I've been reading from Kant to good use, raise an unusual topic, and see what happens*, I thought. *Perhaps God could use it to get us talking about things that matter more than good pizza.*

As a question began forming in my mind, doubts started to creep in as well. *He's going to think I'm really weird — and so will my wife and our new friends.* But I also thought it was strange that he was just standing there, as if he was waiting for something to happen.

"Yes," I piped up cheerfully. "I have an important question."

"Great!" he replied. "What is it?"

"I've been reading Immanuel Kant, and I was wondering," I said with feigned curiosity, "do you think that the categories of the mind apply to the noumenal world in the same way they apply to the phenomenal world?" (I was fairly sure I knew what I was talking about, but at any rate I felt safe that he wouldn't know one way or the other.)

He looked at me, surprised. Then he smiled and shot back with a spirited tone, "I'm not sure, but I once heard about a scientist who looked through his telescope and thought he saw God. Pretty strange, huh?"

"That's not at all strange," I said, amazed at his response. "I don't know if this was the guy you heard about, but I recently read a really interesting book by a well-known scientist named Robert Jastrow, called *God and the Astronomers*. It was his observation of the incredible order and intricacy of the universe that led him to finally conclude that there must be a God. His book shook up a lot of people in the scientific community."

"Wow, that's interesting," he said. "I really don't think about God too much. What did you say the name of that book was?"

Suddenly, we were off to the races in a fascinating spiritual conversation. Before I knew it, I was explaining some of the scientific evidence that supports our Christian beliefs, and a couple of us described the difference Christ had made in our lives.

We eventually got around to figuring out what kind of pizza to order, but I don't remember much about the food that night. What stands out in my mind was the surprising discussion we had and how it all resulted from what felt at the time like a crazy impulse to throw out an unusual remark.

Our interactions didn't end with that encounter. I asked him if he would be interested in reading Jastrow's book, and he said he would. So a few days later I brought him my copy, along with a couple of other smaller books I thought would provide good answers to some of his spiritual questions.

He seemed sincerely grateful for the information. And although I never had the chance to interact with him after that, I'm glad I took a little risk that night by tossing out a playful and unexpected question. As a result, look what happened: on an evening when we were anticipating only a quiet informal dinner, the four of us got the chance to tell someone about Jesus, and I was later able to put some potentially life-changing materials into his hands.

Who knows how God will ultimately use this impromptu interaction in his life? It makes our hot and spicy pizza — as good as it was — seem bland by comparison.

> Action Principle

God wants to use your unique personality. Take courage, have some fun, and let your lighthearted side out. Be your own eccentric self and let the adventure begin.

> Stepping into the Adventure

One of the greatest enemies of the unexpected adventure is our insistence on always expressing ourselves within the bounds of Christian normalcy. So we end up dressing, looking, talking, and acting like a hundred other people in our church, fearful to express our true individuality and possibly stymieing our unique ability to connect with people in our circle of influence.

As if God were the creator of clones.

He tells us in Psalm 139:14 that we have been "fearfully and wonderfully made." And one verse earlier, we read, "You knit me together in my mother's womb," which includes not just our bodies but also our personalities, temperaments, and unusual styles — quirks and all. God made *me to be me* and *you to be you*, and he wants to use each of us within the special designs he has given us.

Think about it: there are people in your world who don't know Christ and who need to see him expressed through your full and untethered personality. These folks are as colorful as God made you to be, but they may not relate to you as long as you're playing it safe and masking the full expression of your authentic character.

"Dare to be a little eccentric," psychologist Alan Loy McGinnis said in his popular book *Confidence: How to Succeed at Being Yourself.*[3] When I consider the magnetic people I know, most of them tend to be a little offbeat, unafraid to express themselves in fresh, unusual, and sometimes surprising ways. Just being around them is to experience the *unexpected*. Their personalities give them an infectious influence on others.

> Relax. Open up. Be more playful. Try some humor and laugh at yourself if it doesn't work. Be your own eccentric self.

That night in the pizza parlor, God used my individuality to open doors to an important conversation. How might he want to use you in daring and out-of-the-box ways?

Take a moment right now to pray for the courage to express the full personality God gave you. Ask that he would open doors of influence through which you can express yourself for him, guided by the Holy Spirit.

Then relax. Open up. Be more playful. Try some humor and laugh at yourself if it doesn't work. Be your own eccentric self — and watch God use you in extraordinary ways.

> Inspiration for the Journey

Therefore, since we have such a hope, we are very bold.

2 Corinthians 3:12

THOSE IMPERFECT OPPORTUNITIES

LEE STROBEL

It's the telephone call nobody ever wants to receive: "Mr. Strobel," the doctor said, "we have the results of your biopsy. I'm afraid it's cancer."

I can tell you from firsthand experience what happens at the moment you hear those incendiary words: your mind flashes to the worst-case scenario and instantly you find yourself contemplating your own mortality.

I was fortunate; my cancer didn't end up threatening my life. Nevertheless, the frightening experience of hearing that initial diagnosis left an indelible impression on me. Like never before, I was prompted to think about how my behavior would change if I knew I only had a short time to live. And that is what brings me to the story about Tim.

Tim and I became buddies after he moved into my neighborhood in the seventh grade. As fairly close friends for the next half dozen years, we spent long hours shooting baskets on the driveway, playing softball at the park, and talking incessantly about girls, cars, and sports. Mostly girls.

Did I mention girls?

Except for my occasional rants against Christianity, which were fairly common back in my teenage days as a budding atheist, I don't think we ever discussed spiritual matters. Tim and his family didn't go to church, although he didn't seem as hostile to religious faith as I was. He was simply indifferent toward God.

After high school we left for different universities. Unlike today, with the advent of text messaging, email, and cell phones, friends at that time often drifted apart when they went away to college, and that's what happened to Tim and me. Many years later I heard through the grapevine that he was working for a large corporation, living in a distant city, and had gotten married but subsequently went through a divorce. In the meantime, I had lost my faith in atheism and become a Christian.

Then came the news that Tim and his new wife were moving to a city not far from where I was living. I was ecstatic: maybe we could reconnect and I could talk with him about Jesus.

But I wanted to do things right. First I was determined to renew and deepen our relationship, and then I would broach the topic of faith at the perfect moment, after trust and credibility had been established. *There's a lot at stake*, I thought. *I want to look for the ideal opportunity so I don't blow things.*

Leslie and I invited Tim and his wife over to dinner. Over a meal of barbecue chicken, we chatted about the Chicago Bulls, the Chicago Cubs, and the Chicago Bears — or, as we Chicagoans call them, "Da Bulls, Da Cubs, and Da Bears." On other get-togethers, Tim and I watched sports on television. I kept looking for the perfect opportunity to bring up God, but I never felt the setting was quite right. Once we were too engrossed in a game; another time his wife was there and I wanted to talk to him when he was alone.

Then one day he called with the urgent news that he had been transferred to a city on the other side of the country. He had to leave right away. Suddenly, both Tim *and* time were gone, and in our busyness we again drifted apart.

I was kicking myself. Surely I could have found some way to bring up the most important topic in the world to someone I really cared about. I recalled the advice my mother had given me when I got married: "If you wait until the perfect time to have children," she said, "you'll never have them." And by insisting on the perfect time to broach a spiritual conversation, I ended up never having it.

A while later I heard that soon after Tim had moved, he became friends with a Christian who rather promptly engaged him in a spiritual discussion and invited him to his church. Unbeknownst to me, Tim was primed for God, and he immediately and enthusiastically received Christ.

I was thrilled when I heard the news. At the same time I wondered when I ever would have found that elusive ideal moment to have the same kind of conversation with him. In fact, long after he became a Christian, Tim confessed to me that he wondered why I had chosen to remain silent for so long about something as supremely important as the gospel.

> By insisting on the perfect time to broach a spiritual conversation, I ended up never having it.

Patience is important in personal evangelism. We want to validate the seeking process of others, and we don't want to push someone any faster than he or she is able to go. All that is fine, but if we go too far, waiting for that absolutely perfect opportunity to talk about Christ, then there's a good chance we'll never get around to talking about spiritual matters at all.

If I lived with my own mortality in mind, however, surely things would be different. If I knew I only had a short time to live, there would be a new urgency injected into my evangelistic efforts. I would probably be more up front about spiritual matters. I wouldn't wait endlessly for those ever-elusive ideal circumstances before I talked to others about Jesus. Let's face it: those perfect moments rarely come anyway.

More often, if we're alert to opportunities and attuned to the Holy Spirit's promptings, we're going to find some appropriate way to get into a conversation about Jesus. It may not be the ideal circumstance, but if we approach the situation with sensitivity and empathy, chances are that God will take our meager efforts and use them in the life of our friend.

Because the truth is, we don't have all the time in the world — and even more important, our friends don't either.

> Action Principle

If you wait for the ideal moment to bring up spiritual matters to others, you'll probably never get around to it. Be patient but also persistent. Keep in mind that God can take imperfect opportunities and use them for his perfect purposes.

> Stepping into the Adventure

My friend Kerry Shook and his wife, Chris, wrote a best-selling book called *One Month to Live* in which they encourage Christians to focus on how their priorities and attitudes would change if they only had thirty days left in this world. Certainly this kind of perspective would affect how we spend our time and resources, what we choose to say — and not say — to others, and what we value most highly. It also would prod us along the evangelism continuum, from too much *patience* on one end toward greater *urgency* on the other.

Most of us naturally tend toward the side of patience. But sometimes we can linger for so long on that end of the spectrum that nothing happens, as I did with my friend Tim. Of course, none of us wants to overcompensate by going overboard on the urgency side, where we become pushy and even obnoxious to the point of chasing people away. Yet good intentions aren't enough.

So here's a good experiment: for the next thirty days, why not live as if this were your last month on earth? In what practical ways would this change how you engage with people about God? How far might you inch along the continuum toward the urgency end? You might want to keep a journal about your experiences or make this an activity for your small group or Sunday school class.

> Why not live as if this were your last month on earth? In what practical ways would this change how you engage with people about God?

After all, our days *are* limited. As Kerry said:

> No matter how much this idea makes you squirm, it's fact. No matter who you are, how young or old, what measure of success you've attained, or where you live, mortality remains the great equalizer. With each tick of the clock, a moment of your life is behind you. Even as you read this paragraph, seconds passed that you can never regain. Your days are numbered, and each one that passes is gone forever.[4]

Kerry doesn't see this as depressing. "I'm convinced," he said, "that rather than inhibiting us to play it safe, embracing our time on earth as a limited resource has incredible power to liberate us."[5]

That is, we can become freed up — with new vigor and enthusiasm — to find creative ways to bring the news about the God we love to the people in our lives that we love as well.

❯ Inspiration for the Journey

Teach us to number our days and recognize how few they are; help us to spend them as we should.

Psalm 90:12, TLB

EMBARRASSED FOR GOD

MARK MITTELBERG

We were on a ministry trip to England, serving a church on the south side of London for an entire summer. Our goal was to meet people at their homes throughout the neighborhoods, share the story of Jesus, and invite them to the church.

Knocking on doors and talking to strangers about God has never been my cup of tea, even in a land where everybody drinks it. Thankfully, I had my wife, Heidi, with me; she is outgoing and gregarious (not to mention *attractive*) and thus was able to open more doors than I ever could have.

The Londoners we talked with were generally polite but usually not very interested in discussing spiritual topics. Frankly, it was tough going. "You have an American accent," one said. "Why don't you go home and pester people in your own country?" It was clear that many of these folks were very private about religious matters, and some were pretty jaded after previous visits from people who tried to recruit them into various cults.

The people most open to discussions were newcomers themselves to the area, usually immigrants from overseas. One couple was particularly receptive. Yash and Sanya had moved to England only a couple of years earlier. They immediately welcomed us, apparently happy to get to know some new friends.

Yash and Sanya were wonderful people, natives of a small island in the Indian Ocean that I'd never heard of called Mauritius. When I asked them where it was, they explained that Mauritius was just off the east coast of Madagascar. And when I asked them where Madagascar was, they told me it's an island off the east coast of a much larger island — called Africa. (I was pretty sure I knew where *that* was.)

After meeting a couple of times and having some great conversations, Sanya invited us to return a few days later for an authentic Mauritian meal. We had no idea what that would be like, but it sounded like a culinary adventure, and it would provide us more time to get to know our new friends.

When we arrived they greeted us at the door, seemingly honored that we would come and spend time with them. We were impressed that they went to so much effort to prepare such an elaborate homemade meal.

Before we ate, Heidi and I sat for a while in a side room, chatting with Yash. Suddenly he left the room, and when he reappeared he was holding what was a very special bottle of champagne, a gift to be served to their important guests.

I wrestled with how I should respond. I didn't want to offend him, but at the same time I didn't want to offend the church we were there to serve, which frowned on drinking alcohol in any form. I remembered the apostle Paul's admonition to "eat whatever is put before you without raising questions of conscience" (1 Corinthians 10:27), but decided to try taking a middle road.

I said, "Yash, that's something you've been saving for a really big event; you don't need to open that for us. Why don't we just have juice or water?"

Yash wouldn't hear of it. I'd hardly gotten my words out

when he jubilantly exclaimed, "I've been saving this for a day like today — when I can honor special friends like you." With that he began to pry off the cork.

Now it was quite warm in their apartment, and Yash may have jostled the bottle when he took it down from the rack. Whatever the cause, the cork came out with a powerful "pop" and the bottle erupted, *spraying half of its contents all over me.*

I stood for a moment in shock. Champagne was dripping from my hair, off of my face and glasses onto my shirt, soaking into my jeans. I felt like a large sponge and smelled like a winery.

Uncomfortable as I felt, I tried to regain my composure and laugh it off — but Yash was horrified. "*Sorry, sorry, sorry, sorry,*" he kept repeating as he stood staring at me, his face aghast, trying to figure out what to do.

"Come upstairs with me so I can dry your clothes," Yash finally instructed. I wasn't sure how he planned to do that, but I didn't have any better ideas, so I compliantly followed him up the steps.

"Give me your trousers," he said as he got out an iron and an ironing board. Our wives were downstairs, and it was a fairly private setting, so I dutifully took them off and handed them over to him.

I sat in a daze as I watched Yash crank up his iron to its highest setting and then proceed to singe my new Levis in an effort to dry them quickly. My pants sizzled as plumes of steam rose and the smell of burned champagne filled the room.

How in the world did I end up here? I asked myself, clad in my underwear, while my friend diligently worked to dry my clothes and restore my dignity. *I'm just trying to serve you, Lord,* I said silently, and *look at what I'm going through.*

> *I'm just trying to serve you, Lord, I said silently, and look at what I'm going through.*

I won't claim that I heard an audible response from God, but I did have the impression that he was speaking to me: *You're there because you love me and because you care about this man and his wife, both of whom I love deeply. You're there in the effort to obey and serve me, and I will honor you for that. And, yes, you're feeling uncomfortable right now, but don't get too glum about it. You're not suffering in a serious way. In fact, if you'll just relax a bit, you'll realize that it's pretty funny.*

It was then that the real humor of the moment hit me. I resolved to lighten up, breathe deeply (ignoring the smell of burned alcohol and smoldering denim), laugh at myself, and be a friend to my buddy Yash. Soon, with a new perspective and wearing warm and (mostly) dry jeans, I went back downstairs, where we all enjoyed a delicious meal and had one of the most encouraging spiritual conversations that Heidi and I engaged in all summer.

I don't know how Yash and Sanya will finally respond to our message. But chances are we'll all remember — with smiles — our great time together on that unusual evangelistic summer adventure.

> Action Principle

For many Christians, life is plain vanilla too much of the time. There's nothing necessarily wrong about how they're spending their time, but there's nothing really exhilarating about it either. Another day, another yawn. But start taking some risks to share your faith and watch the *excitement* return with its ups and downs — perhaps even a few awkward but memorable moments along the way. So often, personal evangelism is the missing ingredient to living a life of true adventure.

Stepping into the Adventure ◂·····

Jesus said that in this world we will have trouble (John 16:33), and certainly he went through incomprehensible amounts of it while fulfilling his divine mission. Paul echoed Jesus' thoughts in 2 Corinthians 11, where he detailed the hardships he endured in order to reach the world for Christ. His list includes things like whippings, beatings with rods, a stoning by an angry crowd, several shipwrecks, including treading water for a day and a night, and frequent sleeplessness, hunger, and thirst. It's a list that makes me feel embarrassed about feeling embarrassed in the story I just told.

Thankfully, the worst thing most of us followers of Christ in the Western world will experience as we share our faith is inconvenience and perhaps occasional ribbing or ridicule from the people around us. Maybe even a rare case of outright rejection. But that shouldn't shatter our world, should it? Isn't it worth it for the sake of reaching people so loved by God?

Don't you sense that there's nothing better than being, as the Blues Brothers famously put it, "On a mission from God"? What could be more important? I'll tell you this: nothing is more exciting or rewarding than being out on a limb with God, trusting and serving him. *That* will spice up your Christian life.

> Nothing is more exciting or rewarding than being out on a limb with God, trusting and serving him.

So lift up your eyes, catch God's vision for the people in your world, step out in faith, and watch the Holy Spirit work through you. Besides, you'll have a lot more interesting stories to tell.

› Inspiration for the Journey

But he said to me, "My grace is sufficient for you, for my power is made perfect in weakness." Therefore I will boast all the more gladly about my weaknesses, so that Christ's power may rest on me.

2 Corinthians 12:9

BREAKING THE PACT

LEE STROBEL

When Leslie and I moved to a new community, we sat down and discussed how we could strategically reach out to our neighbors with the message of Jesus. We would try to be attentive to ways we could serve them. We would drop hints early that we were Christians in order to plant seeds for future spiritual conversations. We would endeavor to follow a godly lifestyle so we might be "salt and light." When we took our evening strolls together, we would silently pray for our neighbors as we walked by their homes. And we thought we had a pretty good game plan until God reminded us that a big part of the adventure of evangelism are the surprises he brings along the way.

One day I saw a neighbor I hadn't met. He was busy washing a car in his driveway, and I could tell by the lack of license plates that he had just purchased it. Seizing the opportunity to get to know him, I walked over and congratulated him on his purchase.

> We thought we had a pretty good game plan until God reminded us that a big part of the adventure of evangelism are the surprises.

49

"You picked a great car," I told him. "The auto magazines have given it excellent reviews."

"Thanks," he replied with a smile, using a chamois to soak up water from the car's silver hood.

He seemed personable and extroverted. Soon we were embarking on a lively conversation that went from cars to families to basketball. Before long, our chat turned to one of my favorite topics: restaurants.

"Did you see the barbecue place that just opened?" I asked.

His eyes lit up. "No, but I *love* barbecue. Where is it?"

"Not far."

He glanced at his watch. It was about 5:15 p.m. "Let's get the wives and go over there right now," he said.

"Great idea. Can we take your new car?"

"Sure," he replied, clearly happy to show it off.

I hurried back to our house and found Leslie getting ready to start cooking dinner. It didn't take much persuasion to convince her to go to the restaurant instead.

"This guy seems really nice," I said. "This is a good chance to get to know him and his wife. But let's not push God on them. I don't want to seem overbearing and scare them away. Let's just have a nice dinner, get to know all about them, and see if this might be the start of a real friendship. Then when the opportunity arises in the future, once we have a solid relationship, we can bring up spiritual matters."

Leslie nodded. "Okay, let's make a pact."

"Right," I replied. "We won't bring up church or religion or God or Jesus or faith or any other spiritual topic tonight. This is merely a get-to-know-you kind of thing." At the time, it seemed like a good plan.

We clambered into the backseat of his car and took off toward the restaurant, our new friend and his wife in the front. It was a temperate evening, so we rolled down the windows and were enjoying the light breeze and even lighter conversation.

A couple of minutes later we drove past a sign announcing that a new church was going to be constructed at the corner of an intersection not far from our houses.

"Hey, look, they're going to build a church there," my neighbor observed, gesturing out the window.

"Hope it's one of those cute places with a steeple and everything," his wife added. When our secret pact kept Leslie and me from commenting, she added, "We don't go to church ourselves, but I do think spiritual stuff can be fascinating. You know, Oprah and all."

I bit my tongue.

A red light stopped us at the edge of the quaint downtown area. An elderly Catholic priest, wearing a clerical collar, passed in front of the car as he ambled across the street.

"Don't you think priests have gotten a bad rap?" my neighbor commented, taking a quick look at Leslie and me in the rearview mirror. "Just because of some bad ones, people forget all the good things the church has done for people — like in the inner city. They do baseball leagues and help keep kids off the streets. I don't believe in God, but I'm glad there are religious people doing some good stuff in the world."

Leslie and I exchanged glances, then mumbled something noncommittal in response.

His wife filled the silence. "I grew up Catholic," she added. "Went to parochial schools. What bothered me the most was that we didn't read the Bible very much. I think that's a shame. I would really like to understand it more, but a lot of it's really confusing to me."

She turned, putting her elbow on the top of the seat so she could look at us more directly. "Have you folks read the Bible at all?"

That did it — the pact was off!

How ironic: there we were, two evangelical Christians in the backseat, hesitant to bring up spiritual issues because it might frighten our unchurched friends into thinking we wanted to strong-arm them about faith, while those same friends were blithely making repeated references to church, spirituality, the Bible — and they didn't want to let the topic go.

Leslie and I jumped into the conversation, and all through the rest of the ride and during what turned out to be a pretty tasty meal of barbecue ribs, we had an animated discussion about a range of spiritual topics. It was the beginning of several other important God-related conversations we would have with our neighbors before we ended up moving away to another community.

The lesson was simple but important: people are generally more interested in spiritual matters than we think they are. For the most part, they have opinions about church, religion, God, and Jesus, and they're more than willing to talk about them. As long as we're respectful and truly listen to their point of view, many of our friends and neighbors would probably enjoy discussions about faith.

Especially if the barbecue is good.

> Action Principle

Christians often assume that they would need to drag an unchurched person, kicking and screaming, into a conversation about spiritual matters. On the contrary, spirituality is a hot topic these days. People like to offer their viewpoints and compare them to yours. So don't fall into the trap of self-censorship. Daily life is full of opportunities to engage people about God.

Stepping into the Adventure ←······

The statistics may surprise you: according to pollster George Gallup, eight out of ten Americans say religion is at least fairly important in their daily lives.[6] Public-opinion researcher George Barna has found that among *unchurched* Americans, one out of five reads the Bible and nearly seven out of ten pray in a typical week.[7]

When *Time* magazine faced a news drought a few years ago, they threw an article about Jesus on the cover, and the issue became their biggest seller of the year. Books about God — pro and con — pepper the best-sellers lists. I've found that my atheist friends bring up the topic of faith more often than most Christians I know.

> Now more than ever, it's socially permissible to get into conversations about faith — if we do it sensitively.

The reality is that people are intrigued by spiritual stuff. Now more than ever, it's socially permissible to get into conversations about faith — if we do it sensitively. For example:

- *Find a natural way to segue into spiritual topics.* If you're talking about the upcoming weekend, you might say, "I'll be watching the ballgame, washing the car, and going to church this weekend. By the way, do you ever think about church or God very much?" Or around Christmas or Easter, you could say, "What holiday traditions did your family follow when you were young? Did they include church? Do you ever go now? What prompted you to stop going?"

- *Listen, listen, listen.* Let your friend dominate the initial conversation. Ask follow-up questions — and then ask more questions. Take an authentic interest in his viewpoint. Empathize with his feelings wherever possible. Don't jump in and correct misstatements about the Bible or Christianity; you can always discuss those later. As we respectfully listen to our friends' opinions, we earn the right to offer our own beliefs, whether then or later.

• *Pray for the Holy Spirit's guidance.* Ask him to help you discern what to say, when to say it, and how to express it.

Oh, and one more thing: relish the adventure.

> Inspiration for the Journey

Be wise in the way you act toward outsiders; make the most of every opportunity. Let your conversation be always full of grace.

Colossians 4:5 – 6

SPUR-OF-THE-MOMENT FRIENDSHIP

MARK MITTELBERG

I was rushing to pick up a few things at the grocery store so I could get home before the afternoon was completely gone. I should have known better; I can never find what I'm looking for in grocery stores, and trying to hurry doesn't help. Somehow, though, I finally managed to hunt down all the items I needed, and I headed toward the lines of people waiting to make their purchases.

On my way toward the cash register, a display of freshly cut flowers caught my attention. *This is perfectly placed to appeal to weak men so they'll bring home flowers to their wives,* I mused. However, I also noticed a strikingly beautiful bouquet that Heidi would be sure to like. *And being the weak person that I am,* I thought, *I think I'll take* this *one. She's gonna love it.*

Picking up the flowers, I turned to the lines at the tills, calculated the quantity of groceries in each person's cart, and estimated the efficiency of each cashier. Then I placed my bet by getting in what appeared to be the fastest moving line.

My private "race-to-the-registers" game was interrupted, however, when I noticed the elderly lady standing in line in front of me. She looked friendly and ready to talk to pass the time, so we struck up a conversation, discussing nothing in particular. As we got up to the register and started to take items out of our carts, she noticed my bouquet.

"I remember when my husband used to bring me flowers," she said wistfully. "But he died many years ago."

It was obvious she still missed him, even after all these years. I said what I could to try to cheer her up until she paid for her purchases, and then we said good-bye.

She left the store while the cashier was ringing up my items, when suddenly an idea struck me: *give her Heidi's flowers*. I felt torn at first, wondering how Heidi might feel about it. But I knew she would care far more about encouraging a sweet elderly lady than she would about getting flowers for herself.

So I hurriedly paid for my things, rushed outside, and spotted the woman walking across the far end of the parking lot. I ran to catch up to her, holding out the bouquet as I got closer.

"Your husband isn't available to do this," I said, suddenly feeling a bit shy, "so I'd like to give you these ... for him."

Her reaction told me it had been some time since a younger man had chased her or given her flowers. Surprised and delighted, she said, "Oh, thank you very much! That's so kind of you ... and so much like something my husband would have done."

She asked how my wife was going to feel about losing her flowers to a complete stranger. I told her I thought Heidi would be more than happy to make this small investment in her happiness. We continued to chat for a while, when I realized there were no vehicles parked nearby.

"By the way, where is your car?" I asked.

"Oh, I don't drive," she said. "I live just six or eight blocks from here, and with this good weather, it's not hard for me to walk."

"Well," I replied, "I've already given you the flowers — the least I can do is give you a ride home."

"Oh, you don't need to do that," she said with a pause and a twinkle in her eye. "But if you really want to, I'll invite you in for a pot of my favorite tea and show you a few pictures of my husband too. He was quite a man ..."

"I'll bet he was," I answered. Obviously, God had a different plan for my afternoon than I had. "And tea sounds great. My car is over here."

I gave her a ride, went in and had some tea — which, as my British friends would say, was *lovely* — and saw the pictures and heard the stories about her husband. Soon she became curious about me, my wife, and what it was that had caused a young businessman to go out of his way "for an old lady like me."

I assured her she didn't look that old, and I told her I thought that God might have prompted me to give her the flowers. I explained that I had trusted my life to Christ not too many years earlier, and that he was slowly turning me into the kind of person who would care about the needs of others.

I didn't preach, but I gently shared what I had learned and experienced, and I encouraged her to consider the gospel for herself. We had a great conversation, and it led to several other spiritually oriented interactions later on (some of which included Heidi, who, by the way, was pleased when she heard the story about her flowers). I don't know what my friend's final conclusion was concerning her relationship with God, but she certainly did listen in an open and intent way.

> I didn't preach, but I gently shared what I had learned and experienced.

A decade later, after Heidi and I had moved several times and were living in another state, this lady went to the effort of finding our new address and mailing us a package that included gifts for our kids and a letter telling us how — ten years after we had first met — she often told friends about my act of kindness and how it had blessed her that day. Amazing how one small gesture can touch a heart — and hopefully open it to the love of the Savior.

> Action Principle

It's an old but true statement: people don't care how much you know until they know how much you care. In other words, our message of love has much more impact when it's preceded by our acts of love. So as you prepare to share the gospel with the people in your world, pray also for the opportunity to *show* them the gospel, remembering that truth plus kindness is a winsome combination.

> It's an old but true statement: people don't care how much you know until they know how much you care.

> Stepping into the Adventure

St. Francis of Assisi is believed to have once said, "Preach the gospel at all times — when necessary, use words." It was a poignant way of pointing out that our daily actions are important and need to convey God's message of love.

The apostle James presented the idea with a challenging question: "Suppose a brother or sister is without clothes and daily food. If one of you says to them, 'Go in peace; keep warm and well fed,' but does nothing about their physical needs, what good is it? In the same way, faith by itself, if it is not accompanied by action, is dead" (James 2:15 – 17 TNIV).

The lesson is clear: what we *do* really does matter.

As you live your life today, be mindful that even the smallest of acts can have the biggest of consequences. Watch for opportunities to offer a kind word, to extend a hand to a neighbor, to assist a child or an older person, or to lighten the load of someone weighed down by the burdens of life. Pray that God will show you ways you can exhibit his love through acts of sacrifice and service. Then when you see an open door, be sure to go through it.

But let's not forget the flip side of the coin. The Bible also asks, "And how can they believe in him if they have never heard about him? And how can they hear about him unless someone tells them?" (Romans 10:14 NLT).

In effect, God's Word completes the truth of what St. Francis said by reminding us that words *are* necessary. We must do more than silently serve people, hoping they'll somehow notice the spiritual dimension in our lives. For them to really understand and embrace our message, the apostle Paul warns that we'll need to explain it to them verbally as well.

So a second lesson is also clear: what we *say* really matters too. Therefore we need to look for ways to lovingly serve others and explain to them the message of God's love. Actions *and* words together are two of our most valuable tools in this unexpected adventure.

Inspiration for the Journey

Dear children, let us stop just saying that we love each other; let us really show it by our actions.

1 John 3:18 NLT

PUTTING LOVE INTO ACTION

LEE STROBEL

Leslie and I burst into tears — and I mean that literally: we *erupted* into sobs when the grim-faced doctors broke the news to us at Leslie's bedside. There was something terribly wrong with our newborn daughter.

Alison was being rushed into the hospital's neonatal intensive care unit. The doctors needed our signatures on legal documents to authorize emergency tests. We were told to prepare for the worst. We were devastated and gripped by fear. *Why her? Why us?* It was the worst nightmare of every parent.

Alison's sudden illness shocked us because everything had seemed fine the first day of her life. Although Leslie's labor had been unusually long, the birth itself was uneventful and the baby seemed to be healthy, alert, and content.

Like all new parents, Leslie and I got caught up in the excitement and euphoria of the long-anticipated event. I remember calling relatives from the recovery room. "You know how most newborn babies are all wrinkled and ugly?" I would say. "Well, Alison's not like that. She's absolutely beautiful!" (Now when I look at old photos of Alison moments after she was born, she looks just like any other infant who had just struggled through birth. But such are the eyes of a new father.)

Then, the following day, Leslie and I were waiting for the nurses to bring Alison for her one o'clock feeding. But they didn't come. We were starting to get impatient. Finally, just before I was going to find out what was holding them up, there was a knock at the door. In came a contingent of doctors bearing the terrible news that made our hearts jump into our throats.

The next several days were a stomach-churning blur. It was agonizing to see our firstborn child hooked up to machines and monitors, with an intravenous needle in her ankle. What's worse, we weren't Christians at the time — and without God, there was really nowhere to turn.

In the midst of that horror, I was walking in despair down the hospital corridor when a telephone on the wall rang. A nurse picked it up and then looked around. "It's for you," she said.

On the line was David, a man I had known years earlier but hadn't seen in a long time. At first I was puzzled why he would be calling me, especially there. The truth is that in the course of interacting with David in the past, I had lied to him, misled him, made fun of him, broken promises to him, and ruthlessly criticized his church and everything it stood for. But he was a committed Christian, and that's why he was on the phone that day.

"I heard what's going on with your little girl," David said, his voice laden with concern. "What can I do for you? Can I come down there and be with you for a while? Would you like to talk? Can I bring you anything? Can I run some errands for you? Lee, just give the word and I'll be there as soon as I can. In the meantime, I'll be praying for your daughter, and so will my friends at church."

I was incredulous! I couldn't believe he had bothered to track me down and was willing to drop everything, take time off from work, and drive sixty miles just to help me. Or that he and some strangers in a church were willing to get on their knees and plead to their God for the recovery of a child they had never met — the offspring of an avowed atheist, no less. There's no way in the world that I deserved that.

I thanked David, although I didn't take him up on his offer. Then after ten tense days, Alison simply recovered from her mysterious illness. The doctors didn't know what to make of it and, by God's grace, to this day she has never exhibited any lingering effects from it.

Since then Leslie and I have tried to forget the trauma that we went through when Alison was hospitalized. Yet today, more than three decades later, I could take you back to the precise spot where I received that call from Dave. That's how deeply it's seared into my memory. His unselfish willingness to serve us was one more influence in my own journey toward Christ.

David's actions illustrate the kind of impact that Christians can have when we're willing to go beyond mere words and put the love of Christ into practical action. After all, talk is cheap. Look at Jesus: he didn't just *say* he loved the world, he *showed* his love by becoming a servant.

Jesus served the blind by restoring their sight, lepers by renewing their health, sinners by forgiving their wrongs, and even wedding guests at Cana by turning water into wine. Then in the greatest act of servanthood in history, the Son of God willingly sacrificed his life in order to open the doors of heaven for anyone who would trust in him.

When we serve others as Jesus would, when we sacrifice for others as Jesus did, and when we put our love into tangible action as Jesus modeled, then this can open the hardest of hearts that would otherwise be impervious to the message of Christ. Jesus told us in Matthew 5:16 that if we serve others with "good deeds," they will be prompted to "praise your Father in heaven." That's because when we make the choice to sacrifice our time, energy, or finances to help someone in need — that is, when we act against the grain of our narcissistic, me-first culture — then people will be curious about what motivates us. Their eyes will naturally drift toward our heavenly Father, who is prompting us to live out the kind of compassionate lifestyle that his Son exhibited.

Words evaporate quickly. Most of what a pastor says in a sermon will be forgotten before dinner. But people remember a selfless act of servanthood forever. To use Jesus' metaphors of salt and light, few things are as savory or illuminating as a simple act of kindness performed in the name of Jesus.

> Most of what a pastor says in a sermon will be forgotten before dinner. But people remember a selfless act of servanthood forever.

I can attest to that because I'll never forget David.

> Action Principle

If you want to inject some adventure into your life, use your "compassion radar" to scan the lives of your neighbors, colleagues, and other people you encounter. Detect their needs and then seek out opportunities to serve them. Your sacrifice on their behalf will be an example of what Jesus is like, and there's a good chance they're going to want to know more about the One who motivates you.

> Stepping into the Adventure

Is there an elderly widow down the block who needs someone to go to the grocery store for her each week? Or a junior high student who's looking for someone to shoot baskets with him? Or a single mother who could use a baby-sitter for her two children every once in a while? Or a disabled veteran who needs someone to clear the snow off his sidewalk? Or a colleague who's going through a divorce and could use a listening ear over lunch?

Opportunities to serve others are all around us; we just need to ask God to open our eyes to the situations where he wants us to get involved. You'll be surprised at how easily and naturally spiritual conversations flow when people feel sincere gratitude for the help you've provided them.

I remember flying into Midway Airport in Chicago late at night during a blizzard several years ago. An engineer from India was sitting next to me. As we talked, I found out he was planning to take a bus all the way to O'Hare Airport and then have his pregnant wife drive down from a distant suburb with his two young children to pick him up. To me, that sounded like a formula for frustration.

"Look, I have a car at Midway," I told him. "How about if I give you a lift home?"

He was very grateful, and during our drive through the snow-storm, he asked why I had been willing to go out of my way for a stranger like him. I tried to explain by saying, "Has anybody ever done something so kind for you that it makes you want to pass a kindness along to someone else?"

He thought for a moment and then nodded slightly.

"Well, here's the thing," I said. "Jesus Christ has done something incredibly kind for me."

As we talked, he began to understand how God's outpouring of grace had motivated me to help him. When we finally arrived at his house, he braced for the cold as he stepped from the car. "I'm going to have to do some thinking about all of this," he said as he thanked me and said good-bye.

There's no doubt in my mind: my *words* about Jesus registered with him because he experienced the *love* of Jesus through my practical deed of giving him a ride through a storm.

The truth is that even the simplest acts can have an eternal impact.

> Inspiration for the Journey

In the same way, let your light shine before others, that they may see your good deeds and glorify your Father in heaven.

Matthew 5:16 TNIV

INVITING ADVENTURE

MARK MITTELBERG

"Hi, Mark. Remember me?"

I wanted to say yes. I strained my memory in an effort to say yes. I opened my mouth hoping to get out a yes. But I couldn't honestly say the word.

"Umm, you're going to have to help me out a bit," I said to the young woman standing in front of me by our church's pond, her hair dripping wet.

We had just completed our annual June baptism service, and by God's grace, hundreds of new believers had stepped into the water to affirm their commitment to Christ and their desire to make that reality known to friends, family, and strangers alike.

This was always a highlight of the year for our congregation. For those of us involved in the evangelism ministry, it was our ultimate celebration — sort of like Christmas, Easter, and birthday parties all wrapped into one. It was the visible manifestation of a year's worth of prayers and relationship-building, spiritual conversations and inviting friends to our church's holiday events, weekend services, small groups, and special outreach gatherings.

I had a personal tradition of marking what happened at that service each June. I would arrive early and find a place to sit on the rocky shore of the lake, as close to the action as possible without getting my feet wet. Then I'd snap pictures using a telephoto lens, just before or after people went down into the water.

In particular I'd watch for individuals I knew, especially those whose spiritual journey I'd been personally involved with. It was my way of recording the results of some of my own outreach efforts, even when I was just a small link in the chain of influences the Holy Spirit had used to lead the person to faith in Christ.

Usually I would remember at least the faces, if not the names, of the people whose lives God has used me to help reach. But that was not the case with the woman who was standing in front of me.

"We met four years ago when you and your wife were looking for an apartment in Streamwood," she explained. "I worked for the rental company that was showing the apartments. I walked you through the models we had available. I thought you guys seemed pretty interested, but then you never came back."

"I'm sorry, we ended up in another area west of the church," I said, still trying to reach back into the dusty fringes of my memory. I could recall the apartment complex and the tour of the layout options, but not much about the actual conversation with her.

"That's okay," she said. "You did what you were sent to do."

"We did?" I said, feeling a mix of curiosity and relief.

"You sure did. Don't you remember that you started telling me about this church? You told me it was a great place to meet new friends and to learn about the Bible."

"It's starting to come back to me."

"You also gave me one of those little business card – sized invitations to the church. Remember, it had a map on it?"

"Of course — I try to carry them with me all the time," I replied, silently deepening my resolve to continue the habit.

Our church printed those cards so everyone in the congregation could carry them in their wallets or purses. This made it easy to invite folks to the church by placing something in the person's hand that would give them the essential details, including the church's name, address, and phone number, the times of the services, and a little map of the church's location on the back. Today, of course, the cards also include the Web address so people can check out the ministry online before coming to visit.

I always found it easy to carry and give out these cards to anyone who might be interested, especially around major holidays when people were more likely to visit a church. What I liked about them was that they didn't overreach or try to sell anything. In other words, they didn't open up and play the chorus of "Amazing Grace" or try to present "six easy steps to get to heaven" within their two-by-three-inch space, something that might be technically accurate but appear simplistic to serious seekers. Instead, they merely communicated the essentials about the church, making it clear that it's a place where visitors are welcome.

"God used that conversation and another one soon after it with someone else to get me to visit this church," she continued. "Then after I had attended for a while, I began to understand the message. I finally asked Jesus to forgive my sins — and today I was baptized! When I saw you out here during the service, I decided I should come over to reintroduce myself and update you on what has happened. Thanks for letting God use you!"

"You're more than welcome," I said enthusiastically, feeling dazed but thrilled by the unexpected news. I gave her a hug and congratulated her once more as I thought out loud: "This is really amazing!"

This young woman's experience was a great reminder to me

that day — and I hope to you today — of the big ways God can use each of us when we're willing to take even a small step to reach out to someone who might not know him.

> Action Principle

We often make outreach harder than it needs to be. We figure we can't do *anything* until we're ready to do *everything*. So instead we do *nothing*, hoping someone else will do the job. As a result we miss both the adventure and the spiritual impact. Instead, we need to take small steps to point people in the right direction whenever we can. In other words, do *something* and see how God might choose to work through it.

> We often make outreach harder than it needs to be. We figure we can't do *anything* until we're ready to do *everything*. So instead we do *nothing*.

> Stepping into the Adventure

It's not necessarily our task to invent the ball, produce the ball, transport the ball, and track the ball's every movement. It's just our job to get the ball rolling.

Very rarely will we be involved in a person's spiritual journey all the way from point A to point Z, and it's crushing if you think that you must be. Some people believe it's their sole responsibility to get to know every person, cultivate their spiritual curiosity, invite and bring them to church, answer all conceivable spiritual questions, explain the nature of God (including, of course, every facet of the Trinity) as well as all the details of the gospel, lead them in a prayer of commitment, baptize and disciple them, and then follow through and make sure they get ordained into the ministry and sent away to the mission field. Listen: if you can pull off that chain of events regularly, then I want to read *your* book.

Seriously, God does want to use us in various ways on that seemingly daunting list, but rarely on all of them and virtually never by ourselves. A big part of why he has given us the church is so that we have partners in this grand outreach adventure. As a body we can combine our efforts to pray, serve, and communicate in order to help people see, consider, and choose Christ.

In addition, our gatherings, when planned and led in ways that show "wisdom toward outsiders, making the most of the opportunity" (Colossians 4:5 NASB), can be spiritually contagious places for people to visit. They provide a setting where we can bring our friends to see the love of God lived out among our members and expressed in our worship of him. They allow the truth of the gospel to be communicated in a clear and uninterrupted fashion, from a leader who is gifted to teach and prepared to do so with excellence. They can communicate the subtle but vital truth that our message makes sense and impacts lives, evidenced by the believers who are present, serious about learning, growing, and serving God and each other as well as the world around them.

In sum, our gatherings can provide an environment where, as Jesus put it, "everyone will know that you are my disciples, if you love one another" (John 13:35 TNIV).

So with all that evangelistic potential, one small thing we can do is to invite people into our gatherings, whether for regular church services, small groups, classes, or special events. Just ask, and who knows what God might do with it. Years later you might have someone walk up to you after a baptism service, dripping wet, ready to give you a hug and a heartfelt thanks.

> Inspiration for the Journey

And the lord said unto the servant, Go out unto the highways and hedges, and compel them to come in, that my house may be filled.

Luke 14:23 KJV

EMERGING FROM THE COCOON

LEE STROBEL

The sun was scorching. I found a patch of shade under an expansive tree and sat cross-legged on the brown and brittle grass. I was visiting the predominantly Hindu province of Andhra Pradesh in southeast India as a volunteer writer for an Indian ministry. My task was to produce articles about the thousands of people who were crowding into exciting nighttime rallies to hear the message of Jesus.

But today was something new: an American pastor was going to stop by and speak at a modest event in a sparsely populated farming community at noon, when it was hot and people were generally busy in the fields. Frankly, I was skeptical that anybody would show up.

Half a dozen Indian musicians began playing music to attract a crowd. I picked up a tambourine and tried to keep the beat of the syncopated tunes. (Thankfully, nobody captured this on video, and YouTube didn't exist yet.) Soon some onlookers began to gather. Fifteen minutes later, there were twenty-five people sitting on the grass, apparently curious why anyone would come to this remote and seemingly forgotten locale.

The musicians played song after song, nervously looking around for the pastor. He was late and there was no sign of him. The people were getting antsy; the music could only keep them from going back to their fields a little while longer. Finally one of the musicians bent down and whispered to me, "One more song, then you give the sermon."

I glared at him. "*Me?*" I nearly shouted in a panic. I was a journalist, not a preacher. I had never given a sermon, especially halfway around the world. In fact, I had never spoken about my faith to any group of people. The last time I had given a speech was in high school. I had no notes, no message, no training, and no experience. What I *did* have — in abundance — was paralyzing stage fright. What could I say? How could I speak to these Hindus who were so culturally different from me?

The music stopped. There was absolute silence. Twenty-five pairs of quizzical eyes bored in on me. My palms began to sweat, my knees shake, my heart palpitate. Fighting back waves of nausea, I slowly rose to my feet, my mind churning wildly to come up with something to say as the interpreter took his position, ready to translate my words into Telugu.

"So ..." I began, offering a weak smile, "Hindus, are you?"

The interpreter shot me a perplexed glance as if to say, *Is that really how you want to start?* I was tempted to tell him, "Just deal with it. I didn't *ask* to be up here." But when I didn't say anything, he dutifully translated my words. There was no discernible reaction from the small gathering.

I really can't recall the details of what I said next. I think I talked about Jesus. I'm pretty sure I told them why I loved him

> I had no notes, no message, no training, and no experience. What I *did* have — in abundance — was paralyzing stage fright. What could I say?

and how he had forgiven all of my wrongdoing — past, present, and future. Chances are I told the story of how I came to faith.

When it came time to share the gospel, my mind was a jumble. I tried to remember some Bible verses and give a coherent explanation for Jesus' death on the cross. I attempted to explain why these lower caste Hindu laborers should abandon the only religion they had ever known and risk the rejection of their family, friends, and community by embracing Christ. Instead I simply rambled in disjointed sentences.

I felt like an utter failure. I had an overwhelming and oppressive sense that I had made a complete mess of things. At the end I said something like this: "I know it would be a great sacrifice for you to receive Jesus. I know this can be dangerous around here, so don't even consider it if you're not ready. Believe me, I'll understand. But we're going to play one more song while I pray. Then after you've had a chance to think about it, if you want to put your trust in Christ, I'll help you do that."

I folded my hands, shut my eyes, bowed my head, and, in dejection and despair, offered a silent prayer — of *repentance.*

Oh, Father, I'm so sorry. I know I'm not Billy Graham. I know I'm not qualified to give a sermon. I don't deserve to be doing something this important. I'm sure I botched it. Please forgive me for thinking that a sinner, a nobody, a former atheist like me could represent you to these precious people. They deserve so much better. If you just let me get out of here safely, I promise you I'll never do this again. Please, please forgive me.

With that, I opened my eyes, looked up — and gasped! Twelve men and women had stood to their feet and stepped forward to receive Christ, tears flowing down their cheeks. It was like an electric shock jolted my body. And I knew at that moment that I would never be the same.

If that musician had given me a choice, I never would have

opened my mouth that day. Had there been a graceful way to escape it, I certainly would have. No question, I was unqualified and unprepared.

Yet on that sizzling afternoon in the middle of the grassy countryside on the far side of the planet, God evicted me from my cocoon and sent me soaring on a completely undeserved adventure. I never could have anticipated that within five years of that incident I would be a teaching pastor at one of the largest churches in America, speaking there and around the country to thousands of spiritually curious people.

But God knew.

Who knows what he has in store for you? You may never go to India or give a sermon. But if you ask God to let you experience the electrifying joy of sharing your faith with others, then the day is coming when he's going to gently and lovingly nudge you out of your cocoon. He might ask you to become friends with a spiritually confused neighbor, or share the grace of God with your wayward brother, or tell your book discussion group the story of your conversion, or get into an Internet dialogue with a skeptical blogger.

> I wish I could tell you it won't be scary, but it probably will be. However, I can tell you this: you will never be the same.

I wish I could tell you that when that moment comes you'll feel qualified and prepared, but the chances are you won't. I wish I could tell you it won't be scary, but it probably will be.

However, I can tell you this: you will never be the same. And you will never want to shrink back into the stale safety of your former cocoon.

Action Principle <

You don't know what the future holds, but God does. And sometimes he has to take us there kicking and screaming. On the day when he wants you to graduate to the next phase of the unexpected adventure of evangelism, it's going to seem intimidating. But nothing is safer than being squarely within God's will. So here's some advice: when God wants to stretch you, remember — it's best to be flexible.

Stepping into the Adventure <

He was the weakest member of a faithless family living on the wrong side of town. He had a tentative and doubt-filled personality. And when we encounter him in the Bible, he's cowering out of fear that marauding outlaws might hunt him down.

His name was Gideon. One day an angel appeared to him, and guess how he greeted this quivering coward? He could have called out, "Hey, you yellow-bellied chicken!" or "Hey, you with the spaghetti spine!" But instead, the angel said something entirely unexpected. He declared, "Hey, Gideon, you mighty warrior!"

Why did he call him that? Because God was able to see Gideon not only for what he was but also for what he could become — if he followed God on the adventure that God was opening up for him. And although he would stumble occasionally, Gideon went on to achieve great things for God, and his name has lived on through the centuries to this very day.

So as God looks at you sitting there right now, what might he call out to you? How about, "Hey, you difference maker!" or "Hey, you kingdom builder!" or "Hey, you faithful messenger of my grace!" or "Hey, you effective ambassador for Christ!"

We have no idea where God will take us, and since we don't know what's going to happen, we feel anxiety. But Scripture assures us that we don't go alone. The Holy Spirit is our guide, our encourager, and our equipper. He can give us words when our tongues are tied. He can give us courage when we want to run. And he can use us even when we feel as useless as I did on that hot, humid afternoon in India. Whether it's to reach millions of people or one lonely soul who desperately needs a savior, God has an adventure in store for each of us.

So think for a moment. Imagine what you might become. Go ahead — consider the possibilities. You can be sure of this: God already has.

> Inspiration for the Journey

I can do everything through him who gives me strength.

Philippians 4:13

STUMBLING INTO ACTION

MARK MITTELBERG

I didn't really know what I was doing. I hadn't been through an evangelism course or read any books about unexpected adventures. I felt like a novice when it came to sharing my faith — probably because I was one.

It had only been a couple of months earlier when I had finally committed my life to Christ after years of spiritual drifting. I immediately became involved in the blandly named but spiritually invigorating "Monday Night Bible Study," which consisted of college-age friends who met each week in homes or apartments.

I was attracted to these young and idealistic Jesus-followers because they weren't "playing church" or merely going through the spiritual motions. Instead, they were unashamedly passionate about pleasing God, serving one another, and making a difference in the world.

We viewed the group as a place to grow in our faith as well as to invite friends who weren't Christians. We didn't think much, however, about how our vocabulary, music, or topics of study would be received by the people who visited. We just trusted that our spiritual exuberance would somehow spill over to the newcomers—as it often did.

Looking back, it's clear that God's grace was at work in our guests' hearts in spite of some of our less-than-inviting antics. For instance, we'd bring in friends and then immediately test their spiritual resilience with some of the quaintest religious songs ever sung. To say our tunes were like "Kum Ba Yah" would be less than completely honest; we actually *sang* "Kum Ba Yah" as well as the ubiquitous "Pass It On." All of this among friends who'd grown up enjoying the best of what is now considered classic rock. On top of that, we routinely spoke in "Christianese," debated for hours over obscure theological conundrums, and carried Bibles big enough to warrant their own wheel kits. Still, we genuinely loved God and each other in ways that proved to be infectious to outsiders.

It was into this setting that Peggy, a friend of mine from high school, entered one evening. She had a formal church background, but she hadn't taken it very seriously. Now she was becoming more interested in spiritual matters.

Before we knew it, she was participating in our discussions, singing our songs, even speaking in some of our spiritual clichés. One night before our prayer time at the end of the meeting, she even asked us to pray for her, saying she was drawn to the joy she saw in us and wanted what we had.

Our group was excited about Peggy's involvement, but something kept nagging at me. I couldn't get away from the fear that she was becoming acclimated to our Christian culture but was missing the central point of what it means to become a true follower of Christ.

> Looking back, it's clear that God's grace was at work in our guests' hearts in spite of some of our less-than-inviting antics.

I brought up my concerns privately to a couple of the more mature members of our group. They challenged me not to become judgmental, which I certainly didn't want to be. Yet I couldn't shake my sense of unease, and I prayed that God would show me what to do about it. I wanted to encourage Peggy but thought to myself, *Who am I, a mere spiritual fledgling myself, to be out trying to change somebody else?*

In spite of my doubts and inexperience, God soon answered my prayers for guidance. It was Christmas day, and I was driving down Eighth Street when I saw Peggy walking along the side of the road. I stopped and we chatted briefly, then arranged to meet later that evening to talk further. When we got back together, I told her I was glad that she had been coming to our Bible study. She said she was enjoying it, making some new friends, and learning from the discussions.

"That's great that you're growing in your understanding of God and the Bible," I said, taking a deep breath and trying to act more confident than I actually felt. "But I'm curious to know whether you've ever really asked for Jesus' forgiveness and committed your life to him?"

Her answer struck me in a strong way and has stayed with me ever since. "No, I haven't," she said, "and nobody has ever told me I needed to."

"Well," I replied, "you really *do* need to." Then I did my best to explain what that means. To my surprise, it made sense to her, and we actually ended up praying together, right then and there, to affirm her faith in Christ.

I later found out that God had been working in Peggy's life in a number of ways leading up to that day. He had spoken to her through a Bible she had recently "stolen" from a hotel room (she didn't realize that the Gideons put them there *hoping* people will "steal" them), through a Christmas Eve service at a church the night before, and through several other friends as well as through our group. But what a thrill it was to know God had also used me so early in my own Christian journey to help cement her relationship with him.

That was especially true when, years later, I found out that Peggy (who had since relocated to another part of the country) had married a Christian and they had decided to move to Papua, New Guinea, with their three young children to serve as full-time missionaries. Talk about unexpected adventures! They're still serving there today, though their children are now grown and following God in other places.

Recently Peggy was back in the US, and she had a chance to speak to a gathering of our high school classmates at a school reunion. Here is part of what she said to them:

> At the end of my life I want people to say that I was a good wife and mother, that I was active in my community and things like that. But most importantly, I want it to be said about me that I served God and furthered his kingdom on earth. I want my life to count for something bigger than myself. I want to be able to say that I invested my life well and used the gifts God gave me for his glory.

·····> Action Principle

If you feel less than adequate to be used by God to reach a friend like Peggy, that's probably a good thing. It means you're humble and dependent enough on him, which is precisely what he needs in order to use you. God doesn't need *experts* so much as he needs *servants* — ones who make themselves available and trust that he will honor their efforts to spiritually impact others through them.

God doesn't need *experts* so much as he needs *servants*.

Stepping into the Adventure ←······

In Peggy's message to her former classmates, she said, "I want my life to count for something bigger than myself." Clearly God is fulfilling that desire, in part because she was willing to go wherever he led her and to do whatever he told her to do. In her case, that meant moving to the other side of the world to serve him in ways that have proven both fruitful and fulfilling, not to mention exhilarating.

God using me in this story required far fewer radical steps. I didn't have to leave my hometown, learn another language, or study and prepare for months. I didn't even have to complete a course or read a training manual. Mostly I just needed to cultivate a heart of concern, pray for an opportunity, and be willing to speak up when God gave me the chance. When I did obey him and open my mouth, I'm confident he was speaking through me, using me as part of a whole range of influences that he had orchestrated in Peggy's life.

I wasn't adequate and you don't need to be either because God is more than adequate as he empowers and works through us. Don't get me wrong: I'm all for preparation and training so we'll be able to more confidently share our faith, but that's part of an ongoing, lifelong process. We should take every opportunity we can to learn, grow, and become more effective witnesses for God. In the meantime, however, you need to trust that he will energize and use what he has already given you right now — because he will.

I hope Peggy's story motivates you to take more risks — ready or not — to get in on similar experiences yourself. Reach out to others and open your mouth to speak for God. You might feel awkward and even stumble in your efforts at times, but that's okay. You'll be stumbling into action, and he'll be using you in ways you don't yet fully expect.

> Inspiration for the Journey

For God did not give us a spirit of timidity, but a spirit of power, of love and of self-discipline. So do not be ashamed to testify about our Lord.

2 Timothy 1:7 – 8

FAITH LIKE A CHILD

LEE STROBEL

*Let the little children come to me, and do not hinder them,
for the kingdom of God belongs to such as these. I tell you the
truth, anyone who will not receive the kingdom of God like a
little child will never enter it.*

Jesus in Mark 10:14 – 15

I never fully appreciated what the Bible means when it extols the faith of children — until I met Jack.

Jack lives in a residential facility for the developmentally disabled in suburban Chicago, and every week a volunteer from our church's ministry to mentally challenged adults would bring him to the last of our Sunday services. Jack would always sit near the front, and when the service was over, he would amble over to the pastor who had taught that day and begin talking in a low mumble. His brown hair would be tousled, his clothes disheveled, his tie askew. His face would have stubble and his thick glasses would be smudged.

> I never fully appreciated what the Bible means when it extols the faith of children — until I met Jack.

I didn't know the diagnosis of Jack's condition, but for the most part his thinking was unfocused and his speech was a string of disconnected thoughts. Although he was probably in his late thirties, talking with him was like communicating with a child.

I was a teaching pastor at the church, and after speaking at four weekend services I would be tired when I came off the platform. The line of well-wishers and people with questions was generally long, and at the end of it always came Jack.

Even though I would be exhausted, there was something endearing and refreshing about him. He was so mild mannered, so unpretentious, so unconcerned with what others thought of him. He would inch close to me, dip his head rather than look at my face, and talk ... and talk ... and talk.

At first, I tried tenaciously to follow what he was whispering. Occasionally I was able to discern snippets that made sense to me. Gradually I learned that the best way to interact with Jack was to greet him with an enthusiastic hug, drape my arm around his shoulder, tell him I was glad to see him, and listen ... listen ... listen.

For a long time I wondered how much Jack understood about Jesus. Was he able to follow the sermons? Did he comprehend the gospel? Then one Sunday when Jack came over to me after the service, I saw that his right arm was in a cast and sling.

I pointed to the injury. "Did that hurt?" I asked.

Jack glanced at his arm and then at me. In his halting voice, he replied, "I come here ... and hear ... about Jesus ... and I think about ... all the pain ... he went through ... for me ... and I think ... this was *nothing!*"

I reached out to embrace him. "Jack, that's the most profound thing anyone has said to me for a long time."

There's no doubt that Jack loves Jesus. And what happens when a person truly adores someone? He can't keep it to himself.

So Jack is an enthusiastic participant in the adventure of personal evangelism. He routinely tells the other residents and staff at the facility where he lives that Jesus loves them. He encourages them to visit "my church." (He's very proud of *his* church.)

In his group at the facility, the attendants give each of the residents half an hour a day to play whatever they want on the stereo. Most put on the ballgame or music, but not Jack. He plays recordings of sermons from his church. Can you imagine inflicting my messages on a captive audience like that?

One of the attendants was named Michelle. Over and over, Jack would tell Michelle that Jesus loves her. He would lend her his Christian tapes and invite her to come to church with him. Michelle was deeply touched by his genuine concern for her. After all, she was supposed to be caring for him, and here he was turning the tables. But she didn't take him up on his offers. She kept saying no to him — and to God.

One day Jack concluded that he was getting nowhere just *asking* Michelle to come to church. This time, in his own endearing way, he *told* her, "Meet me there Sunday." He really wasn't demanding it, but he was gently insistent.

Michelle laughed, but she figured, *Oh, well, why not?* Jack was so sincere, so innocent, so full of faith and love and perseverance that she gave in. That Sunday, she sat near the front of the auditorium with Jack. She let the worship music wash over her. She listened intently to the message of grace. She felt her heart begin to open to ideas she had long resisted. And by the end of the day, she found herself saying yes to Jesus.

She later told me how grateful she was that Jack cared enough to persist in reaching out to her even though she had rebuffed him so many times. "Jack," she declared, "is my hero."

How ironic that society treats people like Jack as if they can make no contribution to the world, and yet he has made the single biggest difference that any human being can make in another person's life. The tragedy is that there are so many well-educated, successful, and articulate individuals who will go to their graves never once having made the kind of eternal impact that Jack made when he invited Michelle to church.

Jack did it because he loves Jesus as a little child does: wholeheartedly, unabashedly, and enthusiastically. If we love Jesus in a similar way, then how can we *not* love the people Jesus loves?

Maybe we make evangelism too complicated sometimes. It seems to me that Jack has figured it out pretty well.

⟩ Action Principle

Love is the single greatest outreach strategy because it is the fundamental value that motivates the gospel. When we love God with the guileless heart of a child, it becomes natural for us to tell others about him. So as you embark on the adventure of sharing your faith, nurture your relationship with Christ so that his love for spiritually confused people becomes your own.

> *Love* is the single greatest outreach strategy because it is the fundamental value that motivates the gospel.

⟩ Stepping into the Adventure

Jack made it look so easy, but he didn't do anything that you and I can't do. We can unreservedly love God. We can care about someone who's far from him. We can be as sincere as he is. We can bring up spiritual topics to those around us. We can be tenacious and persistent in a kind and winsome way. We can invite someone to an appropriate service or outreach event at church or in the community. We can ask God to use us, and we can have a childlike faith that he will.

When our daughter Alison was in elementary school, we got

a telephone call asking us to come to see the principal. Leslie and I couldn't imagine Alison getting into any trouble. She was such a well-behaved and considerate little girl.

But we weren't surprised when the principal told us the problem. "It seems Alison is going around to her classmates on the playground and ... well, she's telling all of them about Jesus," he said.

As adults, we could understand how this would be an issue at a public school. But as a child, Alison didn't see any problem with it. After all, if you love someone like she loved Jesus, then you don't keep it to yourself.

No wonder the kingdom of God belongs to such as these—and no wonder Jesus told us to be just like them.

Inspiration for the Journey ◄ · · · · · ·

Brothers, think of what you were when you were called. Not many of you were wise by human standards; not many were influential; not many were of noble birth. But God chose the foolish things of the world to shame the wise; God chose the weak things of the world to shame the strong. He chose the lowly things of this world and the despised things—and the things that are not—to nullify the things that are, so that no one may boast before him.

1 Corinthians 1:26–29

DIVINE INTERRUPTIONS

MARK MITTELBERG

It was supposed to be a quiet meal with Heidi. We were long overdue for a date together, and we needed time to look at our calendars so we could figure out our plans for the upcoming months. We chose a semi-secluded restaurant, arrived after the lunch crowd, and asked to be seated in a private area where we could be alone and talk.

All was good until, fifteen minutes later, a different host seated a couple at the table next to us. There must have been twenty other places he could have put them, but here they were, about an arm's length away in a nearly empty restaurant. I have to admit, I was a bit annoyed.

Heidi and I tried to proceed with our planning, speaking to each other in hushed tones. But as we finished eating, this couple, who frankly seemed more interested in our interactions than their own, finally broke through the invisible barrier and drew us into a conversation.

"So, have you figured out who you're going to vote for yet?" the woman asked.

With all the politeness we could muster, Heidi and I talked

with them briefly about politics, but soon they came around to asking what I do for a living. Taking a deep breath, I explained that I write and speak about faith-related issues from a Christian perspective, and as I spoke it finally dawned on me that God might have a different agenda for this lunch than I had.

> As I spoke it finally dawned on me that God might have a different agenda for this lunch than I had.

As soon as they heard I was involved in ministry, the conversation heated up quickly. "The one thing I'm strongly against is *proselytizing*," the woman declared emphatically as she proceeded — *ironically* — to try to persuade us to her point of view. "Also *missions*," she added. "It really bothers me that missionaries go overseas and ruin people's cultures and destroy their way of life."

I tried to explain that missionaries often help native people in very practical ways that she would probably appreciate. Like teaching them, for example, to stop *eating* each other and to start *loving* each other instead.

She wasn't interested in my explanations. She was too anxious to tell me that she and her husband are ardent atheists, and that they think everyone should have the right to believe anything they want to believe.

I assured her that we agreed: everybody should be free to choose his or her own faith, and we need to be tolerant of those with different points of view. But I explained this doesn't mean that all beliefs are created equal.

She disagreed sharply, telling me that every viewpoint is true for each person (except *mine*, apparently, since she kept disagreeing with it). When I emphasized the need to carefully evaluate the criteria for various belief systems, she again became impatient.

Finally, getting up to leave (her disinterested husband had already paid for their meal and was heading for the car), she stood by our table and talked down to me: "I don't need to study and think about all of that. I've lived my life long enough to know what I believe, and nobody's going to change my mind about it."

I had a feeling she might be right about that last part, and I was tempted to remind her that they were the ones who had dragged us into the discussion in the first place. Thankfully, I restrained myself.

The timing of our conversation was interesting. I'd recently finished writing a book called *Choosing Your Faith ... In a World of Spiritual Options*, and I had just received a few advance copies. In the book I discuss the various ways people land on their particular spiritual beliefs, what I call "the six faith paths."[8]

This woman was a classic example of the first approach, the *Relativistic* faith path. For her, "truth" is whatever ideas a person decides to believe. Since she and her husband are atheists, then for them there really is no God; and since Heidi and I choose to trust in a deity, apparently one exists for us.

Our brief exchange reminded me that we're generally more effective in talking to people about Jesus when we first try to understand how they've come to their current spiritual beliefs and then relate our faith to them in ways they can understand.

For example, I could have presented this woman with all kinds of evidence for the Christian faith, but it would have been like speaking a foreign language to her. Instead, I needed to address her relativism, showing her how this approach fails in every other area of life. *So why believe it in the spiritual realm?* I could have asked her. *After all, what you believe about trucks has no effect on the impact one will have on you if you step in front of it.*

I felt that this discussion, along with the reasons for believing in Christianity that I had written about from science, philosophy, history, archaeology, Scripture, and experience, might really help this woman — but clearly it was too much to discuss at that moment, with her husband waiting impatiently outside.

Then Heidi, exhibiting more optimism than I was feeling, suggested I give her the copy of *Choosing Your Faith* that I had in my computer case. Glancing up and probably sounding a bit skeptical, I said to the woman, "She's referring to a book I wrote that discusses matters of faith and explains how we can make wise decisions about what to believe. I'd be happy to give you a copy if you'd really read it." To my surprise (and after a moment of hesitation), she decided to take both the challenge and the book, and she even asked me to write down my email address so she could later tell me what she thought of it.

I pray that she and her husband will read the book and find the path to Jesus. And I hope that the next time God wants to bring a "divine interruption" my way, I'll be more open and ready for it, realizing that it's just another unexpected excursion in the grand adventure of following him.

> Action Principle

"Adventure" sounds exciting, but "unexpected" sounds ... well ... abrupt and often unwelcome, especially if you're someone who likes to have everything mapped out ahead of time. If that's you, then you may need to loosen your grip on control. Jesus said in John 3:8: "The wind blows wherever it pleases. You hear its sound, but you cannot tell where it comes from or where it is going. So it is with everyone born of the Spirit." In other words, as followers of Jesus, we should start expecting the unexpected.

As followers of Jesus, we should start expecting the unexpected.

Stepping into the Adventure

It's easy to confuse what we've planned for what's really important. The meeting you're in might seem like your top priority, but the unanticipated phone call from your son, daughter, friend, or neighbor might be much more momentous in the long run for both of you.

Isn't it interesting that many of Jesus' most memorable actions were done in response to intrusions into his own plans and schedule? His powerful words to Nicodemus, some of which I quoted above from John 3, came after Nicodemus showed up one night — unannounced and uninvited — to ask a few theological questions. As a result, Jesus was able to seize the opportunity to teach this respected religious leader what it means to experience a genuine spiritual birth and the forgiveness and life that come with it.

Later in John 9 we see Jesus walking along the road (on his way to do important things) when he sees a blind man begging by the side of the path. Rather than viewing him as a distraction, Jesus recognizes a chance to express divine love and compassion. So he stops and heals the man, who immediately becomes a participant in the unexpected adventure himself.

In John 11, Jesus received word that his friend Lazarus was gravely ill. Jesus again changed his plans and made the journey to Bethany. As a result, he not only was able to comfort his friends, who by then were grieving Lazarus's death, but he also performed a miracle, raising this man back to life and, simultaneously, raising the hopes of everyone in the region who saw or heard about his amazing work.

There's no doubt about it: the adventure is as much in the journey as in the destination. So open your eyes today to your surroundings. Become more spiritually circumspect. Yes, do your work, pay your bills, and attend to your hundred daily details. But remember that as a Christ-follower your mission is never just about tasks or achievement.

First and foremost, it's about loving, serving, and reaching the people God places in your life. Their interruptions can become portals into the realms of his supernatural activity and divine impact.

> Inspiration for the Journey

Be prepared in season and out of season; correct, rebuke and encourage — with great patience and careful instruction.... keep your head in all situations, endure hardship, do the work of an evangelist.

2 Timothy 4:2, 5

THE INFLUENCE OF A STORY

LEE STROBEL

He was a hard-drinking, glue-sniffing, drug-abusing, hate-filled urban terrorist who had been in and out of the court system ever since he threw a hammer at someone's head when he was eight years old. He rose to second in command of the Belaires, a vicious street gang that ruled parts of Chicago. And, ironically, he became a significant influence in my journey toward Christ.

How did he do it? As you'll see, Ron Bronski did something that anyone can emulate and that God can powerfully use as we reach out to others.

After various scrapes with the law, Ron got into big-time trouble when he was twenty-one. A member of a rival street gang brutally assaulted one of Ron's friends, and Ron vowed revenge. Soon he tracked down the assailant's brother, whose name was Gary. Ron thrust a gun in Gary's chest and quickly pulled the trigger.

Click.

The gun misfired. Ron pointed the gun in the air and pulled the trigger again; this time it went off. Gary fled down the sidewalk with Ron in pursuit, shooting as he ran. Finally one of the bullets found its mark, tearing into Gary's back and lodging next to his liver. He fell face forward on the pavement.

Ron flipped him over. "Don't shoot me, man!" Gary pleaded. "Don't shoot me again! Don't kill me!"

Without an ounce of compassion or a moment of hesitation, Ron shoved the gun in Gary's face and pulled the trigger once more.

Click. This time the gun was empty.

A siren wailed in the distance. Ron managed to escape the police, but they issued a warrant for his arrest on a charge of attempted murder. With his previous police record, that would mean twenty years in the penitentiary. To avoid prosecution, Ron and his girlfriend fled Chicago and ended up in Portland, Oregon, where Ron got his first legitimate job, working in a metal shop.

By divine coincidence his coworkers were Christians, and through their influence and the work of the Holy Spirit, Ron became a radically committed follower of Jesus.

Over time, Ron's character and values changed. His girlfriend also became a Christian and they got married. Ron became a model employee, an active church participant, and a well-respected member of the community. The Chicago police had stopped looking for him long ago. He was safe to live out the rest of his days in Portland.

Except that his conscience bothered him. Even though he had reconciled with God, he hadn't reconciled with society. He was living a lie, he realized, which, as a Christian, he couldn't tolerate. So after much deliberation and prayer, he decided to take the train to Chicago and face the charges against him.

When Ron appeared in criminal court, I was there working as a reporter for the *Chicago Tribune*. In contrast to the other defendants, who were always offering excuses for their behavior, Ron looked into the judge's eyes and said, "I'm guilty. I did it.

I'm responsible. If I need to go to prison, that's okay. But I've become a Christian, and the right thing to do is to admit what I've done and to ask for forgiveness. What I did was wrong, plain and simple, and I'm sorry. I really am."

I was blown away! Even as an atheist, I was so impressed by what Ron did that he didn't need to approach me to talk about his faith. *I* asked *him* about it.

Over a cup of coffee, Ron recounted his entire story as I scribbled notes. Frankly, his tale was so amazing that I needed to corroborate it. I interviewed his coworkers, friends, and pastor in Oregon as well as the street-toughened detectives who knew him in Chicago. They were unanimous in saying that something had dramatically transformed him. Ron claimed God was responsible. Though a skeptic, I was thoroughly intrigued.

Ron expected to spend two decades behind bars, away from his wife and little girl. But the judge, deeply impressed by Ron's changed life, concluded that he wasn't a threat to society anymore and gave him probation instead. "Go home and be with your family," he said.

I had never seen anything like this. After court was adjourned, I rushed into the hallway to interview Ron. "What's your reaction to what the judge did?" I asked.

Ron faced me squarely and looked deep into my eyes. "What that judge did was show me grace—sort of like Jesus did. And Lee, can I tell you something? *If you let him, God will show you grace too.* Don't forget that."

I never have. Hearing Ron tell me the story of God's transforming work in his life helped pry open my heart to God. Without a doubt, Ron Bronski was one of the key influences in my journey toward faith. Today, more than thirty years later, Ron is pastor of a church near Portland, and we're still friends.

What did Ron do that was so effective in reaching out to me?

He simply lived out his faith and then told me his story. Granted, his was an amazing account. But every follower of Jesus has a story to tell. And here's a counterintuitive secret: you don't need a dramatic account in order for your testimony to influence someone for Christ.

> What did Ron do that was so effective in reaching out to me? He simply lived out his faith and then told me his story.

In fact, sometimes the more mundane stories are the most effective. After all, not many people can relate to the story of a street gang leader turned pastor. But chances are that a lot of folks can identify with a story like yours.

> Action Principle

You've got a story to tell. What was your life like before you encountered Jesus? How did you end up putting your trust in him? How has your life changed since then? You may not think your testimony is sufficiently spectacular, but take heart: people are inevitably drawn to personal stories. God can use even the most routine tale to open the hearts of your seeking friends.

> Stepping into the Adventure

In his book *Come Before Winter*, Charles Swindoll points out that the apostle Paul stood alone six different times in speaking to often hostile audiences between his third missionary journey and his trip to Rome (Acts 22 – 26).

"Do you know the method Paul used each time?" Swindoll asked. "His personal testimony. Each time he spoke, he simply shared how his own life had been changed by the invasion of Christ and the indwelling of his power. Not once did he argue or debate with them. Not once did he preach a sermon."[9] The reason, said Swindoll:

Because one of the most convincing, unanswerable arguments on earth regarding Christianity is one's personal experience with the Lord Jesus Christ. No persuasive technique will ever take the place of your personal testimony.... The skeptic may deny your doctrine or attack your church but he cannot honestly ignore the fact that your life has been changed. He may stop his ears to the presentation of a preacher and the pleadings of an evangelist but he is somehow attracted to the human interest story of how you, John Q. Public, found peace within.[10]

Paul's appearance before King Agrippa provides an easy-to-remember outline for how you can tell your own story. In Acts 26:4 – 11, Paul tells what his life was like before he met Jesus: "I ... [did] all that was possible to oppose the name of Jesus" (v. 9). In verses 12 – 18, he recounts how he encountered Christ: "As I was on the road, I saw a light from heaven ... and I heard a voice." Then in verses 19 – 23, he describes how his newfound faith has transformed him: "So then ... I was not disobedient to the vision from heaven." After recounting his testimony, he then puts the ball in Agrippa's court: "Do you believe the prophets? I know you do," he said in verse 27.

You might be thinking, *Well, here we go again. First an attempted killer becomes a pastor and now Paul hears directly from heaven. My story isn't anywhere near as compelling as those.* The truth is that few people can identify with a brutal street gang leader or the greatest missionary of all time. I've found that a lot of people have difficulty relating to my own story of having been an atheist, since only a small percentage of Americans overtly deny God's existence.

On the other hand, I've seen a lot of people who connect quite readily with the story of my wife, Leslie. She tried to be a good person but didn't really understand God or how Jesus fit into the picture until a Christian friend gently explained the gospel to her. After praying to receive Christ, she has found freedom in God's forgiveness, joy in his presence, and adventure in his guidance.

Dramatic? Not especially. But it's effective because many people can see themselves in her story.

> Don't apologize that you were never an axe murderer who dramatically turned to Christ. Your seeking friends already relate to you or they wouldn't be your friends.

So don't apologize that you were never an axe murderer who dramatically turned to Christ. Your seeking friends already relate to you or they wouldn't be your friends. Tell your story with confidence so that God can use it in their lives. In fact, don't procrastinate: take time today to write out your testimony and practice telling it in three or four minutes. Don't try to memorize it, but get comfortable with what details you want to include and exclude.

Then ask God for opportunities to share it with others — and let the adventure begin.

⟩ Inspiration for the Journey

I have had God's help to this very day, and so I stand here and testify to small and great alike.

The apostle Paul in Acts 26:22

MOUNTAINTOP EXPERIENCE

MARK MITTELBERG

Few places are as beautiful as Montana's Beartooth Mountains in midsummer, and no outdoor activity is more fulfilling than backpacking among the craggy peaks, where the sky is clear, the air crisp, and the aroma of pine needles fresh and fragrant. Then there are the high-altitude flowers, with shapes, colors, and sizes you just don't see down in the lowlands.

One summer, Heidi and I enjoyed a nearly week-long trek into this region. We set up a base camp next to a sparkling mountain stream and took hikes each day, exploring in various directions.

A few days into our trip, we met Dan, who had come up alone and set up camp nearby. We introduced ourselves and invited him to join us the next morning for a day hike up a mountain that overlooked the area. He accepted, and we met him soon after sunrise.

It was a beautiful morning. We walked along, chatting and enjoying the alpine scenery, and the higher we climbed the more mountain flower variations we noticed. After we had all commented about how amazing they were, it struck me that I might be able to bridge the conversation to more significant topics. So I decided to throw out a line and see what happened.

"You know, God must have quite an imagination to create such beauty," I began. "We keep seeing all these incredible shapes and colors of flowers. The Creator must really be creative."

I still have a clear mental picture of the scene: we were on a gentle incline, walking single file on the narrow trail. Heidi was up front, Dan was in the middle, and I was in the back (*somebody* had to guard our group from the grizzly bears). When I made my comment about God's imagination, Dan glanced back at me and said, "Well, I guess that would be true if you believed in God, but I don't."

> "You know, God must have quite an imagination to create such beauty," I began.

End of discussion. Or so he thought.

Dan didn't realize it, but I'm an intellectual-style evangelist who was *looking* for an atheist to interact with in the mountains. *Finally, something really interesting to talk about,* I thought. *Enough about* floral *life; let's talk about* eternal *life.*

It wasn't hard to keep the dialogue going. I simply replied, "Really? You don't you believe in God? Why not?" As I expected, he was more than happy to explain his rationale to Heidi and me.

In fact, the rest of the way up the mountain he did his best to lay out the reasons we shouldn't believe in God, why he couldn't exist, and how we can live without depending on some manufactured deity. We listened patiently, asking a few questions to gain a clear picture of his beliefs and waiting until it seemed right to offer some of our own thoughts.

That opportunity occurred during most of the hike back *down* the mountain. As persuasively as I knew how, I tried to answer the objections Dan had raised and to present what I considered to be compelling evidence for God's existence. We talked about science, logic, philosophy, history, and archaeology, and I tried to explain how all of this — and how knowing Christ in a personal way — had impacted our own lives.

Our discussion lasted all the way back to our base camp, where we started a campfire and talked for a couple more hours. I wish I could report that at the end Dan fell to his knees, confessed his sins, and then begged us to baptize him in the nearby babbling brook as the fish jumped in the warm glow of the late afternoon sunshine.

That didn't happen. I do believe, however, that Dan heard some information he hadn't encountered before. And I trust that God will use that conversation whenever Dan reflects back on our time together.

That said, I think we might meet Dan again in heaven someday. Why? Because there's one more part to our mountain experience.

Heidi and I had to pack up our stuff and head back down the several-mile journey to where our car was parked. We got everything together and stopped to say good-bye to Dan and to encourage him about what we'd discussed.

Then, about halfway down the trail, we stopped at a little stream to rest and get a drink of water. While we were there we met five big, athletic, and very friendly guys heading *up* the trail to enjoy a few days of camping. As we talked with them, we found out they were also Christians — and not just any old Christians; they were leaders in the famed Navigators ministry. In other words, they were sort of like Green Berets for God.

As soon as we found that out, we figured God was up to something — maybe a revival in the Rockies — so we told them about meeting Dan, filled them in on our conversations with him, and even drew them a map so they could locate where he was camping. Then we sent them off with a challenge.

"Look, fellows," I said, imitating the tone of a drill sergeant, "we got this thing started. Now you guys go find Dan and see if you can finish the job."

It might be my imagination, but I think those guys were salivating as they bounded up the trail, swiftly heading toward the spot we had scrawled on that makeshift map.

Now you know why I think Dan might end up in heaven — whether he likes it or not.

> Action Principle

Often the most amazing evangelistic encounters come out of making the right split-second decisions. You might not be thinking about spiritual matters or be aware of the opportunity that's about to open up in front of you. But suddenly you see it and think: *Should I or shouldn't I? I'm not really "prayed up," I don't know what I would say next if the person shows interest, and I'm certainly not ready to answer a lot of deep theological questions.* My advice? Ignore all of that and do four simple things: take a deep breath, say a quick prayer, open your mouth, and let it fly. God can guide and use you, but first you've got to take the small risk of getting the conversation started. That's where the adventure really gets going.

> Often the most amazing evangelistic encounters come out of making the right split-second decisions.

> Stepping into the Adventure

In John 4 we're told about the conversation between Jesus and a woman drawing water from a well. Jesus asked her for a drink, and she quizzed him concerning why he, a Jewish man, would break the cultural customs to talk to a Samaritan woman. But

Jesus wasn't interested in such mundane matters. He saw an opportunity to turn the conversation toward a much more important topic.

"If you knew the gift of God and who it is that asks you for a drink, you would have asked him and he would have given you living water," he told her (v. 10). *Living water? What's that?* the woman wondered. So she started asking him about it.

Jesus had initiated a spiritual conversation, an initial element in the chain of events necessary to fulfill his mission "to seek and to save what was lost" (Luke 19:10). How can we follow Jesus' example? Ask God each day to give you the awareness to *see* the opportunities as well as the courage to *seize* them. Then when you recognize an open door, do the four things I mentioned in the Action Principle:

1. *Take a deep breath.* Funny thing, but outreach always goes best when you have plenty of oxygen in your lungs.

2. *Say a quick prayer.* Ask God to lead and use you. But it must be quick — about the amount of time required to take the deep breath.

3. *Open your mouth.* This makes your words much easier to understand.

4. *Let it fly.* You've got air in your lungs, God on your side, and something to say; what more could you possibly ask for? Speak up and spark some spiritual action. Don't delay, don't change the subject, and don't give the Devil time to whisper in your ear that this is not an opportune moment. Just let it fly, launch into the adventure, and watch God work.

⟩ Inspiration for the Journey

Good people bring good things out of the good stored up in their heart.... For out of the overflow of the heart the mouth speaks.

Luke 6:45 TNIV

LINKING TOGETHER

LEE STROBEL

A person's coming to Christ is like a chain with many links....
There are many influences and conversations that precede a
person's decision to convert to Christ. I know the joy of being
the first link at times, a middle link usually, and occasion-
ally the last link. God has not called me to only be the last
link. He has called me to be faithful and to love all people.

Evangelist Cliffe Knechtle

Vicky Armel didn't look the part. She was an attractive blonde mother of two with a contagious smile and warm personality, but she also had a reputation as being an aggressive and street-toughened detective for the Fairfax County Police Department in Virginia.

A spiritual skeptic, Vicky had little patience when Christians tried to talk to her about Jesus. She would put up her hand and say, "Back up! I don't want to hear it." If they persisted, she would explain that she had investigated many suicides and homicides. "Never once did that dead person get up in three days," she would say.

Then she became partners on a series of cases with Detective Mike "Mo" Motafches, who is a committed Christian (*and link #1 in the chain*). For a year he periodically offered to talk to her about Jesus, but she rebuffed him as she had all the others. Yet somehow Mo's persistence made an impression on her. "He never gave up on me," Vicki recalled later.

> Somehow Mo's persistence made an impression on her. "He never gave up on me," Vicki recalled later.

One day they were sent on an investigation to Maryland, which meant they would be in the car together for five hours. "Okay, this is your time," Vicky said to Mo. "You can talk to me about Jesus all you want, under one circumstance: when we get back to Virginia, I don't want you to talk to me about Jesus anymore."

Mo grabbed the opportunity. He encouraged her to pray and ask God to reveal himself to her. "I guarantee he will answer you if you seek him," he said. Mo talked about the reliability of the Gospels and the fulfillment of ancient prophecies in the life of Jesus against all mathematical odds. And he explained the Bible's central message of redemption through the death of the Son of God.

"Suppose a serial killer is found guilty of his crimes," Mo said. "Then suppose the judge gives him a fifty-dollar fine and no jail time. How would you feel about that?"

Vicky said she would be outraged.

Mo continued. "The payment for the penalty of our sin is so high that only the death of God in the flesh could wipe out the consequences of our sin," he explained. "Imagine the judge found the criminal guilty and sentenced him to death, but then got off the bench, sat in the electric chair, and died in the place of the guilty man. Vicky, God paid the penalty for your sin as Jesus was executed on the cross."

Vicky listened intently but made no commitment. As a trained detective, she needed time to investigate what Mo had explained to her. The very next day she listened to the Bible on CD in her office (*link #2 in the chain*). Mo gave her tapes from his pastor, Lon Solomon (*link #3*), and Christian books (*link #4*). She began listening to Christian radio as well (*link #5*).

"I had never seen anyone so anxious to learn more about God and the Bible," Mo said.

Another friend of Vicky's, Tim Perkins, invited her to Mountain View Community Church on Easter of 2004 (*link #6*), where people warmly welcomed her (*link #7*) and she heard the gospel from pastor Mark Jenkins (*link #8*). The church also gave her a copy of my book *The Case for Easter* (*link #9*), which discusses my examination of the resurrection of Jesus, an event that was the major stumbling block for Vicky. It turned out to be the perfect gift for an evidence-minded detective.

"I read it and read it," Vicky said. "Everything I needed to prove the case for Jesus I found in this book."

Virtually none of the people who were links in the chain of influence in Vicky's spiritual journey knew each other or knowingly worked together to reach her. But each one of them was an influence that God orchestrated to pull her slowly toward the cross. Eventually, overwhelmed by the facts, Vicky prayed to receive Christ as her forgiver and leader.

Mo was there to see her baptized. "What a joy it was for me to watch Vicky publicly dedicate her life to God—a God she once swore didn't exist," he said.

The following year Vicky got up in front of her church to tell the story of her spiritual journey. She began by saying, "My name is Vicky Armel, and if you told me last year that I would be standing in front of hundreds of people talking about Jesus Christ, I would have said you were crazy."

Just one year later, on May 18, 2006, Vicky was working at the Sully District Police Station when she got word there had been a couple of carjackings in the area. She rushed out of the police station to investigate; Mo had been in the midst of addressing an envelope and was just 15 seconds behind her. When she and another officer emerged from the station, they were instantly shot to death by a crazed teenage gunman brandishing an AK-47 assault rifle.

The senseless slayings stunned the community. Mo was grief stricken. "I will miss my partner, my friend, my hero, and my sister in Christ," he said.

But that's not the end of Vicky's story. Nearly ten thousand people — many of them police officers — paid their respects at Vicky's funeral. I'm sure that none of them came expecting to hear from her personally. Yet at the funeral, Jenkins played the tape of the testimony Vicky had given at the church the previous year in which she described her journey from skepticism to faith.

"I know there's probably a Vicky or Victor out there who is searching for God," she said on tape to the hushed crowd. "I hope that my story might help you find God."

And it has. Incredibly, even in death Vicky has become a link in the chain of influence helping to lead many people to Christ. After the funeral, the church received emails and phone calls from spiritually interested inquirers all over northern Virginia. "Some people just walked in off the street," Jenkins said. "They said, 'We want what Vicky had.'"

One person told Jenkins, "It made me rethink my whole life over. I know I've made many mistakes and hurt some people. I want to be saved. I want the Lord in my life. I want him to know that I love him. I'm not sure how to go about doing this. Can you help?"

The unusual nature of Vicky speaking at her own funeral even brought media attention, which spread her story — and the story of her Savior — all over the globe. Who knows how many people will be encouraged to seek Jesus as a result?

A church member by the name of Dwayne Higdon summed it up best. "Vicky didn't just save lives," he told a reporter, "she also saved souls."

Action Principle

Remember that *all* the links in the chain — the beginning, middle, and end — are vital in leading a person to Christ. Most of the time, God uses us as an initial or middle link. Even your smallest gestures — an invitation to church, the gift of a book, an act of kindness in the name of Jesus — can become one of many Christian influences that will accumulate over time in that person's life, hopefully bringing him or her to faith in the end.

Stepping into the Adventure

Too often Christians feel that they have failed if they've never actually prayed with someone to receive Christ. They mistakenly believe that the unexpected adventure of evangelism is confined to that single moment of a person's conversion. Unfortunately, they forget that generally it takes many experiences and conversations over time before a person decides to become a Christian.

I can think of many people whose spiritual input contributed to my eventual decision to follow Jesus. There was the authenticity of my Christian neighbors, the transformation of my newly converted wife, the prayers of my mother, the kindness of a Christian who offered to serve us during our child's illness, the authors of the books I read, the faithful preaching of the gospel at the church I visited, and even the testimony of a convicted street gang leader who shared his newfound faith with me. I'm sure you too can think of numerous links that eventually led you to Christ.

There are opportunities for adventure all along the chain. Our role is to be faithful to God's command to be his ambassadors in a spiritually perplexed world. You may never know how many times God has used you as a beginning or middle link until you get to heaven — and then you will be eternally thankful that you reached out in so many seemingly simple ways to people in your life.

In her testimony played at her own funeral, Vicky had a message for Christians like you and me. "Don't give up on your friends," she said. "Be there for them. Just always talk about Jesus."

And trust that God will use you as one more important link along the way.

❯ Inspiration for the Journey

So neither the one who plants nor the one who waters is any-thing, but only God, who makes things grow. The one who plants and the one who waters have one purpose, and they will each be rewarded according to their own labor.

1 Corinthians 3:7 – 8 TNIV

THE COWBOY WHO ALMOST SHOT ME

MARK MITTELBERG

To call it poor planning would be to give me too much credit. There was no plan at all. It was sheer spur-of-the-moment sanctified stupidity, salvaged only by good motives and a noble purpose.

"I'm feeling wrong about not being with my friends," I told my new Christian cohorts as we sat sipping sodas and eating pizza. "They've been my closest buddies for years and they wanted me to go on the hunting trip with them this weekend. It was a chance to tell them about my commitment to Christ. They're still trying to figure out what happened to me, and I need to talk to them about it."

"Do you know where they're camping?" one of my companions asked.

"More or less, but they left this afternoon, and it's at least a three-hour drive from here," I said, as an idea was born.

"However, if somebody could *fly* me down there," I added, glancing at Dave, "then I could be there in just over an hour." Dave had his pilot's license and we sometimes flew together in single-engine airplanes. "Weren't you just telling me that you needed to clock some air miles?"

"Yeah, but are you *crazy*? Dave protested. "It would be ten thirty before we'd even get started."

"That's never stopped you before," I said.

"Are you serious?"

"I'd like to find my friends," I said, all joking aside. "It'll be an adventure. Let's go for it."

We sprang into action. I rushed home and grabbed my backpack, sleeping bag, tent, and warm clothes. I didn't have time to worry about food, although I did throw a couple of candy bars in the backpack and filled my canteen. *That oughta do*, I assured myself as I raced off to the nearby airport.

Dave and Karen were prepping the plane, and soon we were airborne. As we flew on that starlit night, they started asking me questions: "How are you going to get from the airstrip to where your friends are camping? How will you find them in the dark? What will you do if you can't locate them?"

"Honestly, between the pizza place and here, I haven't had time to figure that all out," I confessed. "I'll hoof it and hitchhike if I need to. God is with me; it's gonna be fun."

We landed on a tiny runway in an unmanned airfield, prayed for safety, and said good-bye. As the airplane took off and disappeared in the distance, I stood there completely alone in a shadowy field near a desolate highway, feeling the midnight November chill of the North Dakota badlands.

Gulp.

"God really *is* with me," I reminded myself, and indeed I could feel his presence. I was a new believer, but I had a quiet confidence that no matter how things turned out, I was in his hands.

I said a quick prayer for guidance and started hiking down the dark highway toward the turnoff to where I thought my friends were.

I soon saw the headlights of a lone car approaching, so I hitched a ride — not something I'd recommend, but the people were friendly and soon dropped me off near where I was headed. At least, I *thought* it was near.

I hiked south down the dusty road at a serious pace. It was much farther than I'd remembered, but no problem, I thought. *I'll stay warm by moving. Besides, I have two Snickers and a canteen full of water. What more could a guy want?*

> I said a quick prayer for guidance and started hiking down the dark highway.

Even when the chocolate was gone and my remaining water had frozen, I wasn't discouraged. I truly sensed God was beside me, showing me he could care for me through my most hare-brained of excursions. I felt his joy as I walked in the moonlight.

But after trekking for miles, I started getting colder and colder. I finally had to admit that I wouldn't be finding my buddies that night after all. I spotted a clearing, climbed a fence, and set up my tent. Before long I was in my sleeping bag, shivering.

I was jolted from my sleep around sunrise. "Who's in there and why are you campin' on my land?" The gruff old rancher's voice boomed through the thin tent wall, sternly warning that I was trespassing and needed to leave — *now*. He talked tough, and what was more ominous, he was packing a fully loaded six-shooter in case of any trouble. In fact, he almost seemed disappointed that I didn't resist.

But as I came stumbling out of the tent, his sympathetic side slowly emerged. "You all alone?" he asked. "You look half frozen. What are you doin' out here?" His crusty demeanor crumbled as I started to explain. Soon he offered me a snack back at his camp.

It turned out his "camp" was an 1800s-built log home and

the "snack" became a hearty four-course breakfast cooked on a wood-burning stove. Over a veritable feast and strong coffee I got to know Ceph, the cowboy who almost shot me, and his wonderful wife, Jesse.

We talked through the meal, poured some more coffee, and kept chatting for hours. He recounted story after story of life on the ranch, blizzards he'd survived, airplanes he'd flown, and wars he'd lived through. I told him about my life, mentioning my freshly found faith and encouraging him to follow the Savior as well.

Soon Jesse brought sandwiches. After eating again, we moved to more comfortable chairs and kept conversing. It was one of the most fascinating days of my life. I'd found new friends and an unexpected opportunity to talk about Christ. God had provided; life was good.

In mid-afternoon Jesse packed me one more meal. Ceph gave me a ride to get my tent and then drove me to an area where many hunters were camping.

"If you can't find your comrades," Ceph instructed, "then find your way back to stay for the night." He pointed out landmarks to help me locate his place. We said farewell and I continued on with my search.

I never located my buddies that weekend. After I finally gave up, I managed to find a ride back home. I did, however, remain friends with Ceph and Jesse, returning to their home several times and corresponding with them over the years.

Today I look back wistfully on that impromptu escapade. The experience reaffirmed for me that life truly is an adventure, that God really is with us wherever we go, and that he is able to bring good out of every situation if we seek to honor him — especially if we don't shy away from the serendipitous encounters he wants to sprinkle into our life along the way.

Action Principle

Predictability is the great enemy of adventure. Planning has its place, but so does God-guided spontaneity. Obviously we need his wisdom and shouldn't do foolish things. At the same time, however, the antidote to a boring Christian life is the willingness to *move* and to let God use us in unusual ways.

> Predictability is the great enemy of adventure. Planning has its place, but so does God-guided spontaneity.

Stepping into the Adventure

What would a truly adventurous person do if he or she were in your place, wanting to reach your friends for Christ? Drive across the country? Book a weekend flight? Buy a book and ship it overnight? Show up unannounced? Offer some selfless act of service? Forgive a trespass? Schedule a party, paying for all the amenities and inviting the entire neighborhood?

I know a woman who did just that. She organized a carnival block party for underprivileged kids, covered the expenses, and gently told them about Jesus. In the end, every child in the neighborhood knew one thing for sure: "that Christian lady" genuinely cared about them.

I know someone else whose dad was near death but living a thousand miles away. Her efforts to share her faith had been unsuccessful, so she arranged to have her pastor fly all the way to her dad's town to visit him. Her plan came together, and it helped her father take steps toward God.

God probably won't lead you to fly into the wilderness, hitchhike into the badlands, camp alone in freezing temperatures, or risk getting shot for trespassing. But who knows? He might. Or maybe he has some other exciting outreach-oriented expedition awaiting you.

Whatever an adventurous Christian might do in your shoes, consider doing that yourself. You might feel stretched and way out of your comfort zone, but Chuck Swindoll was right when he said this in his book *Come Before Winter*:

> Had Christ not taken a drastic step, sinners like us would've never survived the fall. We would never have been rescued. We would be permanently lost. The cross was God's incredible response to our extreme dilemma. Christ did something radical. *Now it's your turn.*[11]

>> Inspiration for the Journey

I have been constantly on the move. I have been in danger from rivers, in danger from bandits, in danger from my own countrymen, in danger from Gentiles; in danger in the city, in danger in the country, in danger at sea; and in danger from false brothers. I have labored and toiled and have often gone without sleep; I have known hunger and thirst and have often gone without food; I have been cold and naked....
I consider my life worth nothing to me, if only I may finish the race and complete the task the Lord Jesus has given me — the task of testifying to the gospel of God's grace.

Paul in 2 Corinthians 11:26 – 27; Acts 20:24

AN UNFAIR
ADVANTAGE

LEE STROBEL

"You Christians are all alike," scoffed the national spokesperson for American Atheists, Inc. "You give the case *for* Christ, but you don't tell the *other* side of the story. Wouldn't it be great if we could lay out the case for atheism, and your side could lay out the case for Christianity, and we could just let the audience decide for themselves?"

Mark Mittelberg and I exchanged knowing glances.

"Let's do exactly that," I declared to the spokesman, Rob Sherman. "You go out and find the strongest defender of atheism you can — your best and brightest. Our church will bring him here from anywhere in the world. We'll go out and get a top-notch proponent of Christianity, and we'll have an intellectual shoot-out."

Sherman immediately agreed. My very next thought was, *I probably should have asked the elders first.* Oh, well, too late. This ball was already rolling, and Mark and I were off to one of the most exciting evangelistic adventures of our lives.

Sherman convinced Frank Zindler, a close friend of renowned atheist Madalyn Murray O'Hair and a top debater for her organization, to represent the atheist side. A former professor of geology and biology, Zindler has vigorously promoted atheism in articles and books and on television and radio programs.

The news media — amazed that a church was unafraid to confront the toughest objections by skeptics — were quickly abuzz.

Mark, who took charge of organizing the debate, asked William Lane Craig to present the Christian case. With doctorates in philosophy and theology, Craig is an author, professor, and one of the top defenders of Christianity in the world.

The debate topic was promptly agreed upon: "Atheism vs. Christianity: Where Does the Evidence Point?"

The news media — amazed that a church was unafraid to confront the toughest objections by skeptics — were quickly abuzz. The *Chicago Tribune* wrote four articles on the upcoming event. Soon I began getting calls from radio stations across the country. "Can we broadcast this debate live?" they would ask. "Uh, sure," I'd say. To our astonishment, pretty soon we had 117 stations from coast to coast.

On the night of the debate, traffic became gridlocked around the church from people flocking to the event. When we opened the doors a full hour before the start time, people ran down the aisles to get a seat. When is the last time you saw someone run *into* a church? In all, 7,778 people showed up, filling the main auditorium and several other rooms linked by video. The atmosphere was electric.

The curtain was about to go up. I was pacing backstage, getting ready to take my position as moderator, when one of the church's leaders walked up to me. "So ... Lee," she said, trying to sound casual, "we are going to win this, aren't we?"

What the public didn't know was that in the basement beneath the stage, a group of Christians had gathered. They were committed to praying during the entire program that the case for Christ would go forth with all of its convicting power and that the case for atheism would be recognized for the bankrupt philosophy that it is.

As they would soon discover, their prayers would be overwhelmingly answered.

Craig began by spelling out five powerful arguments for God and Christianity. First, the beginning of the universe clearly points toward a Creator ("Whatever begins to exist has a cause; the universe began to exist; therefore, the universe has a cause"). Second, the universe's incredible fine-tuning defies coincidence and exhibits the handiwork of an intelligent designer. Third, our objective moral values are evidence that there's a God, since only he could establish a universal standard of right and wrong. Fourth, the historical evidence for the resurrection — including the empty tomb, eyewitness accounts, and the origin of the Christian faith — establish the divinity of Jesus. And, fifth, God can be immediately known and experienced by those who seek him.

Despite Craig's repeated challenges, Zindler balked at offering an affirmative case for atheism. Instead, he charged that biological evolution "is the death knell of Christianity," that there's no convincing evidence Jesus actually lived, and that the existence of evil argues against God.

To the surprise of the audience, Craig promptly used Zindler's arguments against him. He pointed out that if evolution did occur despite the prohibitive odds against it, then it must have been a miracle and therefore it would be additional evidence for the existence of God.

As for evil in the world, Craig said, "No logical inconsistency has ever been demonstrated between the two statements 'God exists' and 'evil exists.' " Besides, he added, in a deeper sense the presence of evil "actually demonstrates God's existence, because without God there wouldn't be any [moral] foundation for calling anything evil." *Touché,* I thought to myself, trying to keep the appearance of neutrality as I sat on stage between the two debaters.

At the end of the two-hour debate and question-and-answer session, I asked members of the audience to set aside their personal beliefs and vote for whichever side had presented the strongest case. It was clear to me that Christianity had thoroughly trounced atheism; the only question was, by what margin? When I was handed the results to announce, I found that a full 97 percent declared that the Christian case prevailed.

A cynic might object, "Well, of course. This took place in a church." However, we also asked people to record their spiritual position *before* the debate and then *after* they heard the evidence. Of the people who marked that they were definitely *not* Christians, an overwhelming 82 percent concluded that the evidence offered for Christianity was the most compelling. And — *get this* — forty-seven people indicated that they had walked in as unbelievers, heard both sides, and were walking out as believers. And not a single person became an atheist.

It was a stunning affirmation of the persuasive evidence for Christianity. After the debate, Mark and I went to his office and collapsed from exhaustion. We had spent many weeks leading up to the event in fervent prayer, never wanting to be presumptuous about the outcome. As we thanked God for the results, this thought came into my mind: *we have an unfair advantage in the marketplace of ideas simply because we have truth on our side.*

> We have an unfair advantage in the marketplace of ideas simply because we have truth on our side.

Action Principle

You may never get involved in a debate between a Christian and an atheist. But you can have a quiet assurance as you engage with your skeptical friends that the evidence of science and history strongly supports your faith. Rather than getting defensive, angry, or unduly argumentative, you can confidently display the "gentleness and respect" that the apostle Peter tells us to have in 1 Peter 3:15.

Stepping into the Adventure

My journalism training wouldn't allow me to take someone else's word for it. The story that came across my desk one day was too big, too extraordinary. As soon as I heard the news, I knew I had to personally investigate it.

Newspapers around the planet were reporting that Antony Flew, one of the world's most prominent atheists, had changed his mind. After fifty years of teaching at Oxford, Aberdeen, and other world-class universities and writing more than a dozen books attacking the existence of God — including *The Presumption of Atheism* and *Atheistic Humanism* — Flew publicly declared in 2004 that he had been wrong. He said he now believes in a supernatural creator.

When I finally got an opportunity to sit down with the white-haired Flew, I found him to be thoroughly likable and engaging. Even at eighty-three, his mind was sharp. When I asked him what evidence caused such a massive shift to his belief in God, he explained, "Einstein felt that there must be intelligence behind the integrated complexity of the physical world. If that is a sound argument, the integrated complexity of the *organic* world is just inordinately greater — all creatures are complicated pieces of design. So an argument that is important about the physical world is immeasurably stronger when applied to the biological world."

Flew is just one of many atheists who have felt compelled by scientific discoveries over the last fifty years to conclude that God exists. I especially like how Flew put it: "I had to go wherever the evidence took me." Even if it was to a conclusion that prompted him to repudiate a lifetime of atheistic scholarship.

Flew's spiritual journey continues. While he isn't a Christian yet, many other atheists — including Harvard-educated Patrick Glynn, author of *God: The Evidence* — have, like me, made the reluctant journey from atheism to faith in Christ based on the evidence of science and history.

What do these stories mean for those of us who are Christians? First, that we can rest easy that our faith in Christ is well placed and can pass every test. Second, that we can have confidence when we have spiritual discussions, knowing there are answers to the toughest objections skeptics might raise. And third, that we don't need to win an argument based on the volume of our voice or the intensity of our rhetoric. In fact, doing so risks the alienation of the very friend we're seeking to reach. Rather, we can present truth in the context of love (Ephesians 4:15), calmly but persuasively explaining why we believe what we believe while modeling Christ's abiding concern for our friend's life and eternity.

> Inspiration for the Journey

Then you will know the truth, and the truth will set you free.

John 8:32

PRAYERS OF DESPERATION

MARK MITTELBERG

I was on a road trip, heading toward the West Coast by way of Montana. I took that route so I could stop to visit friends in several towns along the way. One of them was Lisa in Billings.

Originally Lisa was just the friend of a friend, having dated one of my closest buddies from high school. We met through him but gradually developed our own relationship. So when I made my commitment to Christ a year or so after graduation, Lisa was one of the first people I thought to tell about it.

I decided it would be easiest to call her and explain what had happened, rather than trying to write it all down in a letter. (No, we didn't have email or text messaging back then, but *telephones* were quite common!) I used the phone at my parents' home, assuring them I'd pay the long-distance charges.

I don't know who was in greater shock over the bill that came later for my three-and-a-half hour conversation with Lisa — my dad or me. He just shook his head and gave me the "what's wrong with that boy?" look, but I know he was thankful that at least now my excesses were God honoring, unlike in my days prior to trusting Christ.

I ended up talking to Lisa several times on the phone, and in each instance I sensed spiritual curiosity, but also confusion. It was hard for her to grasp the difference between the Christianity I was describing and the general experience of religion she had growing up. Lisa was raised attending a Protestant church and had never rejected or overtly rebelled against what she'd been taught in her classes, catechism, or the Sunday sermons.

Looking back, I think Lisa was just warm enough toward spiritual things to mask the reality that she was mostly spiritually cold. And while she was a really nice person, there was little in her life to confirm that she was a genuine follower of Christ.

For many months I continued the dialogue. Sometimes I found her fairly open, and other times she didn't want to talk about it at all. During that time my buddy was still dating her, so I went with him a couple of times to Billings. He was pursuing romance, and I was hoping for spiritual impact.

Whenever I sat and talked with Lisa face to face, I sensed she was becoming more receptive. But after I'd head home, I'd soon discover she had slipped back into spiritual neutral. That's why I chose the route through Billings on this particular trip, hoping to talk to her in person one more time.

We sat in her living room, sipping sodas and catching up on what had been going on in our lives. Gradually the topic shifted to God. By this point, however, we were retracing familiar territory. As we talked, it became clear that she was feeling increasingly tense.

"Listen, Mark," Lisa finally blurted out, "I don't understand why you can't just accept me the way I am. I mean, I go to church and I'm a really religious person. It seems like you're judging me, and that there's nothing I can do to convince you I'm okay. Besides, didn't Jesus say we're not supposed to judge people? What makes you any better than me anyway?"

Her words took me aback. "I'm sorry, Lisa," I began, searching for wisdom. "I don't want to be judgmental, and I don't think I'm better than you. But I do care about you and want to try to help you understand and experience all that God offers, because there's nothing better —"

Realizing my response was going nowhere, I abruptly asked Lisa where the bathroom was. She seemed surprised that I needed a break so suddenly, but politely pointed me down the hall. I walked awkwardly out of the room and into the bathroom, where I locked the door and immediately fell to my knees in a prayer of desperation.

> "Please, God, help me get through to Lisa," I prayed. "I really think she's trading religious activities for a real relationship with you."

"Please, God, help me get through to Lisa," I prayed. "I really think she's trading religious activities for a real relationship with you. If I'm wrong, help me see that and to just let it go. But if I'm right, then I need you to intervene somehow ... to open her eyes ... to help me to say the right things to help her finally understand. Please, Father, guide and help me in this, and help Lisa too."

I got up off my knees, regained my composure, and came out feeling much more relaxed and confident. When we restarted our discussion, I sensed that my words were getting through to Lisa with greater clarity. Either way, I knew I had committed the situation to God and that it was in his hands. Soon our time together was over, we said our good-byes, and I left town to continue my journey.

Three weeks later Lisa called me in California. "I finally understand what you've been trying to tell me all this time," she declared, her voice sounding buoyant. "I couldn't stop thinking about it, and to make a long story short, just this week I prayed and gave my life to Jesus. I couldn't wait to tell you!"

"That's amazing!" was about all I could get out before she excitedly continued.

"Thank you for hanging in there for so long, doing whatever it took to help me understand. And that includes," she added with a laugh, "going into the bathroom that night at my house so you could pray for me."

Busted!

"I *knew* that was what you were doing, and at the time it made me really mad," she said. "But you came out acting a lot more boldly and making a lot more sense. So thanks for that too."

And thank God, I thought to myself, that he answers our prayers of desperation — even ones offered from a bathroom floor — as we seek his help in this grand adventure of reaching people for Christ.

⟩ Action Principle

When all else fails — *God is still with you.*

When you lack courage, wisdom, strength, or insights — *God will prevail.*

When you've given up on your efforts and feel you are falling short — *God hears your desperate prayers.*

And when you are weak — *God is at his very best.*

⟩ Stepping into the Adventure

I'm an action guy. And I bet you're an action person too, at least to some degree. We like to figure out what's wrong, come up with solutions, and put our energies into making the needed changes. Then, *when all else fails*, we pray and ask God for help.

Part of that tendency is natural. God created us to be creative problem solvers much like he is. He gave us the intelligence to sort out what needs to be done and the ingenuity to make the right things happen. So when we apply ourselves to fulfill God's purposes in the world, that's mostly a good thing. But if we do so without first seeking his guidance, help, and power, then we're not working wisely and won't have the full impact we might have had.

We often get things backwards. We try, we fail, and then we finally pray. But we need to pray first. As the Bible teaches: pray ahead of time. Then pray along the way. And when things get really tough, pray again with even more intensity. Prayers of desperation, if you will.

We must remember that nothing of enduring value happens on this great adventure unless God is preparing and drawing people to Christ, and equipping and empowering us for our part in communicating his message. As Bill Hybels often repeats, "When we work, *we* work; but when we pray, *God* works."[12] When it comes to reaching family, friends, neighbors, and coworkers, the stakes are simply too

> Let's talk to God about our friends before we talk to our friends about God.

high to go solo — we need to pray and make sure God is working first. Then we can join him, working in tandem with his activities in the lives of friends and loved ones.

So here is today's challenge: let's talk to God about our friends before we talk to our friends about God. Try to do it in that order, but either way, let's keep talking to both, trusting God will do his work.

> Inspiration for the Journey

Now to him who is able to do immeasurably more than all we ask or imagine, according to his power that is at work within us, to him be glory in the church and in Christ Jesus throughout all generations, for ever and ever!

Ephesians 3:20–21

REPRESENTING JESUS

LEE STROBEL

Maggie had been poisoned against God and the church, the result of people who professed faith in Christ but who caused her harm when she was growing up. Here is how she described her experience in a letter to me:

> The Christianity I grew up with was so confusing to me even as a child. People said one thing but did another. They appeared very spiritual in public but were abusive in private. What they said and what they did never fit. There was such a discrepancy that I came to hate Christianity, and I did not want to be associated with a church.

When I read that, I could hardly contain my anger. This was a textbook example of how inauthentic church members can repel people from God. It was a tragedy that someone like Maggie could be deterred from experiencing Christ because of "cosmetic Christians," whose skin-deep spirituality looks pretty on the outside but doesn't penetrate deep enough to change their behavior and attitudes.

Then Maggie read in the newspaper about an upcoming debate

between a Christian and an atheist that I would be moderating at our church. *Perfect,* she thought. *Here's a great opportunity to see an atheist triumph over a Christian.* But to her dismay, the opposite happened. She was stunned to see that the Christian offered persuasive arguments for belief in Christ, which the atheist was never able to refute.

Her curiosity piqued, Maggie began to cautiously venture into our church. She wrote me long letters listing lots of questions about God and the Bible. I did my best to answer them, but finally I told her: "Maggie, I think you could benefit from joining a small group in which several seekers get together with a couple of Christian leaders to investigate faith issues." She readily agreed.

A while later, Maggie wrote another poignant letter. In it she provides a rare window into what the Maggies of the world are looking for in Christians like you and me. As you read it, note the qualities she was desperately seeking:

> So when I came to Willow Creek [Community Church] and to my small group, I needed gentleness. I needed to be able to ask any question. I needed to have my questions taken seriously. I needed to be treated with respect and validated.
>
> Most of all, I needed to see people whose actions match what they say. I am not looking for perfect, but I am looking for real. *Integrity* is the word that comes to mind. I need to hear real people talk about real life, and I need to know if God is — or can be — a part of real life.
>
> Does he care about the wounds I have? Does he care that I need a place to live? Can I ever be a whole and healthy person? I have asked questions like these in my group. And I have not been laughed at or ignored or invalidated. I have not been pushed or pressured in any way.
>
> I don't understand the caring I've received. I don't understand that the leaders don't seem afraid of questions. They

don't say things like, "You just have to have faith" or "You need to pray more." They don't seem to be afraid to tell who they are. *They seem genuine.*

Maggie ended her letter with a poem she had written to the Christians who led her group. The first time I read it, though, I realized that this was something every Christian should read. Please soak in its heartfelt sentiments. Imagine that Maggie is speaking directly to you because, in a sense, she is:

Do you know
do you understand
that you represent
Jesus to me?

If you care,
I think maybe He cares —
and then there's this flame of hope
that burns inside of me.

Do you know
do you understand
that when you treat me with gentleness,
it raises the question in my mind
that maybe He is gentle, too.
Maybe He isn't someone
who laughs when I am hurt.

Do you know
do you understand
that when you listen to my questions
and you don't laugh,
I think, "What if Jesus is interested in me, too?"

Do you know
do you understand
that when I hear you talk about arguments
and conflict and scars from your past,
I think, "Maybe I am just a regular person
instead of a bad, no good little girl
who deserves abuse."

If you care,
I think maybe He cares —
and then there's this flame of hope
that burns inside of me
and for a while I am afraid to breathe
because it might go out.

Do you know
do you understand
that your words are His words?
Your face is His face
to someone like me?

Please, be who you say you are.
Please, God, don't let this be another trick.
Please let this be real.
Please!

Do you know
do you understand
that you represent
Jesus to me?

Tears welled up in my eyes when I first read that poem. I felt the sting of regret over times spiritual seekers had looked at my life and not seen Jesus. I grieved for those occasions when my callousness, indifference, or just plain busyness may have slowed someone in his or her spiritual journey. And I resolved once more just to be genuine with God and with others.

Maggie's words were so powerful that I wanted to read them to our entire congregation, so I called to get her permission. "Maggie, I loved your poem," I said. "Would it be all right if I read it at the services this weekend?"

"Oh, Lee," she replied, "haven't you heard?"

My heart sank. What now? Had she encountered another inauthentic Christian who had chased her away from God?

"No, Maggie," I said with trepidation, "I haven't heard. Tell me what happened."

Her voice brightened. "No, Lee, it's *good* news," she declared. "A few nights ago I gave my life to Jesus!"

I almost jumped out of my chair. "Maggie, that's terrific!" I exclaimed. "But I'm curious about what brought you across the line of faith. What piece of evidence convinced you that the Bible is true? What facts did you uncover that finally established for you that the resurrection was real?" After all, those were the kind of intellectual issues that played a big part in leading me to faith.

> Spiritual seekers aren't looking for perfection in the Christians they encounter. But they do want authenticity.

"No, it wasn't like that for me," she replied.

"Then what was it?"

It was as if she shrugged over the phone. "Well," she said, "I just met a whole bunch of people who were like Jesus to me."

I sighed. What a lesson for me and every other Christian: after Maggie heard the evidence for Christianity in the debate, what she needed most was people who were like salt and light to her — just as Jesus intended in his amazing strategy that is still managing, after two thousand years, to change the world one life at a time.

Action Principle

Spiritual seekers aren't looking for perfection in the Christians they encounter. But they do want authenticity — that is, consistency between their beliefs and behavior, between their character and creed. Unfortunately, when we lack integrity, we give people one more excuse to avoid God. Instead, to use Maggie's word, we just need to be *real*.

> Stepping into the Adventure

When Jesus told his followers to be like salt and light, he meant those as positive metaphors: salt causes others to thirst for God, while light illuminates truth and shines compassion into dark places of despair. But salt and light can have negative connotations too. Salt stings when rubbed into a wound; light causes people to avert their eyes when someone fails to dim a car's high beams on a two-lane highway. In a similar way, inauthentic Christians can cause others to recoil from God.

Before Leslie and I came to faith, we lived in the same condominium building as Linda and Jerry, who were Christians. At the time they probably didn't realize how much we were scrutinizing their lives with our "hypocrisy radar," but we were instinctively trying to discern whether they were genuine.

What we saw was a gentle spirit of acceptance toward us, a lot more humility than pride, a willingness to admit when they were wrong, an anxiousness to reconcile if there was conflict, a readiness to acknowledge the rough edges of their character and a sincere effort to smooth them out, a refusal to playact by pretending that the Christian life was always happy, and an admission that they sometimes struggled with their faith. But most of all, undergirding everything, we saw an honest desire in them to become more like Jesus, bit by bit, as time went by. In Maggie's terms, they were *real*. And as a result, they were both big influences in our journey to Christ.

Now I don't want to make you nervous, but you need to know this: you are being watched. Your friends and neighbors are scanning your life with their own hypocrisy radar because they want to know whether you're authentic. What they observe can either stymie them or propel them forward in their spiritual journey.

So add this reality to your reasons for genuinely and humbly walking with Jesus, day in and day out: your friends, neighbors, and coworkers are counting on it.

Inspiration for the Journey

You are the salt of the earth.... You are the light of the world. A city on a hill cannot be hidden. Neither do people light a lamp and put it under a bowl. Instead they put it on its stand, and it gives light to everyone in the house.

Matthew 5:13 – 15

UNLIKELY CANDIDATE

MARK MITTELBERG

People with many different religious backgrounds lived in the neighborhoods around the church where Lee and I were serving, including a number of Jewish folks. We wanted to reach out to them — respectfully but straightforwardly — and give them the opportunity to hear the claims of Jesus. So we booked the church's main sanctuary, invited a guest teacher, and promoted the event throughout the community.

We called it "A Skeptic's Surprise." The speaker was Stan Telchin, author of a powerful book I had recently read, called *Betrayed!* The book, as well as Stan's talk that night, described the shock he and his wife, Ethel, felt when their oldest daughter called from college to tell them she had trusted in Jesus as her Messiah. *How could this happen,* they had wondered, *to the child of dedicated Jewish parents?*

Stan was so devastated that he suspended involvement in his insurance business long enough to research the facts. He wanted to gather all the information necessary to help his daughter get out of whatever "cult" she had been lured into.

You might guess what happened: the more Stan studied, the

more he became convinced — against his expectations, traditions, and desires — that he needed to take the same step his daughter had taken. Not only did he become a follower of Jesus but in the end his wife and other daughter did as well.

I had underestimated the reaction an outreach event like this could create. Hundreds of people showed up, bringing with them all kinds of questions and challenges. One of those was a Jewish businessman named Don Hart, who felt a mix of curiosity and skepticism as he listened to Telchin's story. Upon leaving, Don couldn't get the message out of his mind. Suddenly he was thinking about spiritual questions he had never pondered before, so he decided to get to the bottom of it all by tracking down one of the event's sponsors: me.

I immediately sensed Don's sincerity when we met in my office. He didn't come to attack what he'd heard; on the contrary, he genuinely listened as I tried to answer his questions. He actually recorded many of my responses in a journal, even jotting down the names of books I encouraged him to read.

When we would get together again, usually a week or two later, he would have one or two of those books with him, the pages already dog-eared and marked up. He always arrived with a fresh batch of questions, and I began to think that if you looked up the word *inquisitive* in the dictionary, there you'd find a picture of Don.

> Jesus said if people seek, they will find, so I kept encouraging myself with the fact that Don was genuinely seeking.

What stands out most in my mind was how Don displayed such intense interest in new and challenging ideas while at the same time harboring such strong resistance to what he learned. The more we met, the greater that tension grew.

I have to admit there were times I wondered — though never

out loud — whether he would ever make a decision. I knew that the combination of Don's skeptical nature and non-Christian background made him an unlikely candidate to embrace Christ. Sometimes I was tempted to give up, but he kept showing interest and always wanted to meet again. I remembered that Jesus said if people seek, they will find, so I kept encouraging myself with the fact that Don was genuinely seeking, so he should eventually get to the finding part as well.

Incredibly, everything culminated when Don started talking about — of all things — attending seminary. At first I thought he was half joking, musing about something he knew he'd never do. That is, until one day when he asked if I would write a letter of recommendation to help him get into a top evangelical graduate school.

"I'd be happy to do that, Don," I responded, "except I think you've gotten things a bit out of order. Don't you suppose it would be a good idea to become a Christian first, *then* consider going to a Christian seminary?"

Don smiled and, with a twinkle in his eye, admitted there was a certain logic to that approach. This led into a conversation about some of the concerns that were still holding up his spiritual progress: Could the messianic prophecies in the Old Testament really point to Jesus of Nazareth? Did Jesus really provide evidence that he was the Messiah? Are there solid reasons to believe in Jesus' miracles — especially the resurrection? Could he, a Jewish man, become a follower of Jesus without losing his identity?

Finally, after a discussion that mostly reintroduced information we had covered previously, Don acknowledged that he had found satisfactory answers to the majority of his questions. Although there would always be more to talk about, he had reached a point of confidence that the evidence supports Jesus' claims. He also understood that he would not be abandoning his

"Jewishness" to become a follower of Jesus. So finally, with joy and anticipation, he prayed with me to receive Jesus as his Messiah and Savior.

Don has been living an exciting adventure ever since that day — one neither of us had expected. Though in his fifties at the time, he enrolled in a program at the seminary, where he rapidly grew in his knowledge of God and the Bible. A couple years later he graduated, and today he works full-time as a biblical counselor, encouraging people in their spiritual development. From time to time he even gets to pray with someone to trust in Jesus, just as he had done.

Recently I called Don, and though we now live many miles apart and hadn't spoken for years, we instantly felt the same spiritual camaraderie we enjoyed back then. The kind that comes from being true brothers in Jesus.

> Action Principle

Who in your life have you written off as "unlikely candidates" for Christ? You may already be saying no for them before they've had every opportunity to say yes to God. Ask God to give you fresh hope and vision for these people and begin to pray and act like he means it when the Bible says, "He is patient with you, not wanting anyone to perish, but everyone to come to repentance" (2 Peter 3:9).

> Who in your life have you written off as "unlikely candidates" for Christ?

> Stepping into the Adventure

I've met flashy Hollywood actors, famous athletes, jaded rock stars, brilliant intellectuals, wealthy corporate executives, and wild-living party animals — as well as one of the most interesting individuals I've ever known, Lee Strobel — all of whom seemed at one time to be highly unlikely characters to become followers of Jesus. Today they're his passionate disciples, eagerly engaging in evangelistic adventures themselves.

Thankfully, someone didn't give up on them but instead kept praying, reaching out, taking risks in conversations, inviting them to outreach events, and loving them even when that got hard. Eventually God's Spirit prevailed and his love broke through. And if *they* can follow Jesus, so can your family and friends who seem so far from him.

Bring to mind people you know but doubt will ever be reached. Better yet, write down their names or print out their pictures and keep these in a private place of prayer. Thinking of these folks one by one, consider:

1. Whether their sins are within the scope of Christ's death on the cross when he became "the atoning sacrifice for our sins, and not only for ours but also for the sins of the whole world" (1 John 2:2).

2. Whether they are included in the group God had in mind when he "so loved the world that he gave his one and only Son, that whoever believes in him shall not perish but have eternal life" (John 3:16).

3. Whether they are some of those about whom God said, "He is patient with you, not wanting anyone to perish, but everyone to come to repentance" (2 Peter 3:9).

4. Whether they are among those Jesus was thinking of when he said, "Whoever hears my word and believes him who sent me has eternal life and will not be condemned; he has crossed over from death to life" (John 5:24).

It's hard to imagine anyone these verses wouldn't include. Notice who the offer goes out to: "the whole world," "whoever," "anyone," and "everyone" who will humble themselves, admit their sin, and turn to Christ.

Why not take steps today to cooperate with the Holy Spirit in reaching out to the people you love and want so deeply to re-spond to the gospel? You've got nothing to lose — and your loved ones have everything to gain.

› Inspiration for the Journey

I am not ashamed of the gospel, because it is the power of God for the salvation of everyone who believes: first for the Jew, then for the Gentile.

Romans 1:16

PRAYING PERSISTENTLY

LEE STROBEL

I'm not sure why I asked the question. Maybe it was natural curiosity. Or perhaps it flowed from my years of experience as an inquiring reporter. Either way, it also seemed to have been prodded by the Holy Spirit.

The day started out as a celebration of God's grace. Hundreds of new followers of Jesus had flocked to our church to publicly affirm their faith through baptism, while their friends, families, and members of the community looked on. Baptism candidates each wore a corsage or boutonniere, and they were told they could invite someone — perhaps a family member or the person who led them to Christ — to accompany them as they walked onto the platform.

I was one of the pastors performing the baptisms, which is always a highlight for me. Few things are as inspiring as looking into the eyes of someone freshly redeemed by God's grace and hearing them affirm their decision to follow Jesus. Sometimes their voice catches as they choke back tears; other times, they can't contain their smile and their face simply radiates gratitude.

A sixty-something woman, wearing a corsage, walked over to

me to be baptized. Next to her was a brawny, tough-looking man who appeared to be a few years older. He looked like a construction worker, his leathery skin deeply etched with lines. I bet he didn't even need a hammer to pound in a nail — he could probably use his fist. I noticed he wasn't wearing a boutonniere.

I turned to the woman. "So, you're here to be baptized," I said.

She was brimming with joy. "Oh, yes, I am," she declared.

I smiled at her answer. "Have you received Jesus Christ as your forgiver and leader?" I asked, although the inquiry seemed merely a formality after I had seen Jesus so clearly reflected in her eyes.

She nodded with enthusiasm. "With all of my heart."

I was just about to baptize her when I glanced at the man at her side. He had been listening intently to what was being said. "Are you her husband?" I asked.

He straightened up. "Well, yes, I am," he said matter-of-factly.

That's when the question popped into my mind. In all of the hundreds of baptisms I have performed, I had never done this before. But for a journalist, this would have been the obvious inquiry to make. So I asked him in a sincere and concerned tone, "Have *you* given *your* life to Jesus?"

He looked surprised and offended. For the briefest of moments, he glared at me. Then his face screwed into a pained expression, and I didn't know what was going to happen. I thought he might hit me. But suddenly he burst into tears, weeping uncontrollably, his shoulders bobbing as he tried to catch his breath.

"No, I haven't," he managed to say between sobs. "But I want to right now."

My knees almost buckled. I couldn't believe this was happening. I glanced around the auditorium, looking for some sort of guidance about what to do next.

"Well, okay then," I finally said. And with that, as thousands of people watched, he confessed that he was a sinner, he received forgiveness through Christ, and I had the privilege of baptizing him and his wife together.

It was a glorious moment in the midst of a soaring celebration. He hardly looked like the same man moments later as he stood next to his wife amidst scores of others who had been baptized as we all sang "Amazing Grace." His smile was as broad and enthusiastic as hers.

Then at the end of the service, just after I stepped off the platform, another woman I didn't know came bounding up and threw her arms around me. As she sobbed on my shoulder, all I could hear her say was, "Nine years, nine years, nine years ..."

As you can imagine, I was a bit flustered. "Excuse me, but who are you?" I asked. "And what do you mean, 'Nine years'?"

She looked up at me, her eyes red from tears. "That's my sister-in-law you baptized up there, and that's my brother who you led to Christ and baptized with her," she explained. "I've been praying for that man for nine long years, and the whole time I've never seen one hint of spiritual interest. But look what God did today!"

Instantly, a thought popped into my mind: *Here is a woman who is glad she didn't stop praying in year eight.*

Yet even as you read that, you might be saying to yourself, *Well, she was only getting started.* Because you've prayed for a wayward son for ten years, or a spiritually confused parent for fifteen years, or a best friend from high school for twenty years. All that time you haven't seen any evidence whatsoever of a spiritual awakening in them. A thousand times, you've been tempted to stop praying for them. What's the use? Nothing is happening. This woman, however, would tell you to *never give up. Never cease praying. Never stop lifting up those you care about to the throne of grace.*

I'll be the first to admit that I don't understand everything about prayer. I know that God lets each person decide whether or not to follow him, and we can't impose our will on someone else, as much as we'd like to. But I'm just naive enough to believe the Bible when it says, "The prayer of a righteous person is powerful and effective" (James 5:16 TNIV).

> Never give up. Never cease praying. Never stop lifting up those you care about to the throne of grace.

In fact, I like the quote popularly attributed to Mother Teresa: "When I pray, coincidences happen. When I stop, they don't."

"Coincidences" such as an inquisitive former journalist baptizing a woman and not being able to resist asking one pivotal question of her husband.

> Action Principle

After getting tired of praying that a spouse, friend, neighbor, or family member would put their trust in Christ, we often give up and go looking for some sort of "evangelistic trick" that might work better. But if the Bible is right when it says that prayer can be "powerful and effective," then our best course of action is to always prioritize prayer, continually asking God to intervene in that person's life.

> Stepping into the Adventure

Have you ever stopped to think that Jesus' prayers for spiritually lost people continued right up until his final breath on the cross? As British pastor John Stott observed in *The Message of the Sermon on the Mount*:

> Jesus seems to have prayed for his tormentors actually while the iron spikes were being driven through his hands and feet;

indeed, the imperfect tense [of the biblical account in Greek] suggests that he kept praying, kept repeating his entreaty, "Father, forgive them; for they know not what they do."[13]

If Jesus prayed for his enemies all the way through the torture of the crucifixion, then isn't it the least we can do to pray for the people we love and care about but who are living in quiet rebellion against God? When we stop praying for people, it's as if we have made up their mind for them. In effect, we're deciding the individual will never commit his or her life to Christ. But how can we possibly do that when so many unlikely people — *myself included* — have unexpectedly ended up in God's family? I'm sure some of my Christian friends had given up on me, but I'm thankful that my wife and God never did.

I remember talking with a man who received Christ as a teenager at an early Billy Graham rally. He tried to convince his stubborn older brother to follow Jesus, but he was continually rebuffed. His brother went on to get a law degree from Harvard and become a highly successful attorney in Los Angeles, steadfastly refusing to consider the claims of Christ. The man told me how he prayed for his brother for forty-eight years and three hundred and forty eight days. He actually counted!

He finally gave his brother a copy of my book *The Case for Christ* on Christmas one year; soon after that his brother was diagnosed with terminal liver cancer. God used the book to appeal to his legal mind, and he ended up committing his life to Christ on his deathbed.

"Did you ever feel like giving up on your brother?" I asked the man who had been praying for him for almost half a century.

The question took him aback. "No. Of course not. He was my brother. I loved him. *What else could I do but pray for him?*"

So let me ask you a question: Who have you stopped interceding for? What person in your life did you once pray for fervently, consistently, and specifically, and yet through the years you've simply stopped? Here's an exercise: bring that individual's face into your mind. Take some time right now to bring him or her to God in prayer, and then commit to regularly intercede for them.

Prayer isn't just one more thing we can do. It's the *very best* thing we can do.

After all, prayer isn't just one more thing we can do. It's the *very best* thing we can do.

> Inspiration for the Journey

The prayer of a righteous person is powerful and effective.

James 5:16 TNIV

ROADSIDE REDEMPTION

MARK MITTELBERG

I hate to admit it, but I was intimidated by Kyle's brilliance. He was one of the smartest students in our high school when we both graduated a few years earlier. I would eventually head off to college, finally becoming more serious about my own studies, but in the interim I stood in awe of Kyle, who knew so much about so many things.

That's why I was surprised when he showed such interest in my newfound faith. Because I so admired him, I didn't quite know how to respond. Fortunately he was truly seeking, so he called one evening and asked if we could get together to continue a spiritual conversation we had begun earlier. I agreed somewhat hesitantly, offering to drive over and pick him up.

I wasn't sure what I was getting into. As I walked into the cool night air, started my car, and began driving toward Kyle's house, I asked God for wisdom. I figured I would need divine help to merely understand Kyle's lofty questions — and then I was *definitely* going to need God's assistance to come up with some good answers.

He climbed into my Camaro, and we decided to just drive

around and talk. This provided a helpful mix of privacy and focus for the conversation, without feeling overly intrusive. I often did this when sharing my faith with friends — especially back then, when gas was cheap.

> We decided to just drive around and talk. This provided a helpful mix of privacy and focus for the conversation, without feeling overly intrusive.

In short order, we were talking about topics he had been studying in college. He tried to explain a particular school of philosophy he had become interested in, but I had never heard of it.

"Exit-stencil-_what_?" I asked him.

"It doesn't derive from the word _exit_," Kyle explained patiently, "but from the word _exist_. It's called _existentialism_, and it was promoted by thinkers such as Jean-Paul Sartre, Friedrich Nietzsche, and even the Christian philosopher Søren Kierkegaard."

"Okay ..." I said, straining to understand what he was talking about. "And how does this relate to your questions about God?"

Kyle took another run at clarifying his position, but I finally decided to try to move the conversation in a different direction. "I'll tell you what, Kyle, you might be able to help me understand this _existent_ ... um, the philosophy you're studying, and then I might be able to offer a few thoughts about some of your questions. But for right now it seems that there's some broader information about Jesus and the central message of the Bible that's important for you to understand. And since I'm fairly new to all of this, I'd like to play you a tape of a talk a Christian speaker gave recently that I thought was really clear and helpful. Okay with you?"

"Sure," Kyle responded.

Relieved, I popped the cassette into my car's tape player (standard equipment back then) and let the recording explain the message for me. That freed me up to simply drive around for forty-five minutes on the rural highways around the outskirts of our hometown as I prayed that the gospel would get through to him.

When the tape finished, I turned off the stereo and let a moment of silence go by to allow the powerful message to soak in. Then I said, "Well, Kyle, what do you think?"

I could tell by the expression on his face that the tape had impacted him deeply. "I've never heard anything like that before," he said with awe in his voice. "That was really powerful."

I was surprised he didn't want to debate anything the speaker had said. Since he seemed so receptive, I decided to ask him point-blank: "Where do you see yourself right now in terms of your own relationship with God?"

His next words amazed me. "I think I need to do what that guy was talking about and ask for God's forgiveness and guidance in my life."

Wow, I thought, *what happened to all of his philosophical questions?* Now that they seemed to have dissipated and God appeared to be at work, I just went with the flow.

"Well, Kyle, it's not really hard to do. I could just pull the car over, and we could pray together right now," I said, as if it were perfectly normal for people to veer off highways at eleven at night and give their lives to Christ. I didn't come right out and say it, but my tone was, *Hey, it's no big deal.*

"Okay, let's do that," he replied.

And we did. I stopped the car on an approach next to the highway, and under the soft glow of the dome light, I led Kyle in a simple prayer. In his own words, he asked for the forgiveness and leadership of Christ. When he said "amen" at the end, I congratulated him on making the most important decision of his life.

Over the weeks that followed, I did everything I could to help

Kyle start studying the Bible, spending time with God, and attending a good church as well as our Bible study group when he was in town. I also encouraged him to talk about his faith with his friends at college. It wasn't too many months later that he told me he had decided to sign up for an overseas ministry stint, where he would have the chance to serve people in a different culture and tell them what it means to follow Jesus.

Kyle left on that trip, and not long after that I moved away as well. I haven't seen him now for years, but I know that when we meet again, he'll be in for the shock of his life when he learns I went on to get my master's degree in — *of all things* — philosophy of religion.

Now I even know what *existentialism* means.

> Action Principle

You don't feel ready to share your faith in certain situations? Welcome to the club. But can you drive a car and maybe play an appropriate message on a CD? Or point your friend to a helpful website, blog, podcast, or effective ministry radio or television program? Or invite him or her to your church, or to a Christian seminar, class, concert, outreach event, or movie? Or give that friend a good book — perhaps *the* Good Book? *Don't let what you think you can't do stop you from doing what you know you can do.* Today's Action Principle is to take some action — today.

> Don't let what you think you can't do stop you from doing what you know you can do.

> Stepping into the Adventure

The unexpected adventure is not something you need to embark on alone. There are a variety of ways, directly and indirectly, that you can partner with other Christians to reach out to your friends.

Matthew, the former tax collector, did this when he "held a great banquet for Jesus at his house, and a large crowd of tax collectors and others were eating with them" (Luke 5:29). If you read between the lines, you see that Matthew wanted to share his newfound faith with his old friends and former coworkers, but he needed some help in the process. So he organized a party that brought them together with Jesus and his new friends, the other disciples. In this way evangelism became a team effort.

The Samaritan woman, after talking with Jesus by the well, seized the opportunity to reach out to her friends in tandem with him. John chapter four says that she "went back to the town and said to the people, 'Come, see a man who told me everything I ever did. Could this be the Christ?' They came out of the town and made their way toward him.... And because of his words many more became believers. They said to the woman, 'We no longer believe just because of what you said; now we have heard for ourselves, and we know that this man really is the Savior of the world'" (verses 28 – 30, 41 – 42). She had done her best to explain the message to them personally, but she knew there was nothing better than letting them hear it directly from the ultimate communicator himself, Jesus.

Here's the simple point: while learning to share your faith, find ways to let other Christians supplement your efforts. Bring your friends to church so they can hear an effective teacher, but if they won't come with you, then find creative ways to bring the church to them. That's something you can do this week, perhaps even today. The results — as I saw when I played the tape for Kyle — can be incredible.

> Inspiration for the Journey

There are different kinds of service, but the same Lord. There are different kinds of working, but in all of them and in everyone it is the same God at work.

1 Corinthians 12:5 – 6 TNIV

SEEING THROUGH SMOKESCREENS

LEE STROBEL

There is a saying in India (*"Sunt vaahate Krishnamaai"* in Marathi) that means people should be as quiet as the flowing of the Krishna River. Sure enough, the river was peaceful and languid when I visited it near the small village of Penumudi in the southeastern part of the country. But on that day I was part of a special mission to stir up these waters that bear the name of a Hindu deity.

Standing on the river's bank, I watched as more than a dozen men and women waded single file into the wide and murky current until they were waist deep. Then one by one, they openly affirmed their decision to follow Jesus and were given a new name from the Bible, as is customary in that region.

With that, they were immersed in baptism by a pastor. The event quickly turned into a joyous celebration, with laughter and tears of joy among the participants and those who gathered to watch. As a journalist sent there to capture the event on film, I snapped shot after shot.

Later that day I was visiting a nearby farming community, where my pale skin quickly drew curiosity from the locals. A young Hindu farmer asked me a question in Telugu. "He wants to know why you're here," my translator said.

With a bit of apprehension, I described the baptism ceremony to him, anticipating that he might react negatively to these people leaving the Hindu faith. On the contrary, he seemed intrigued by Christianity.

"You say these people 'decided to follow Jesus,'" he said. "What does that mean?"

I smiled. "That's a great question." And I proceeded to describe how all the baptized individuals had confessed their wrongdoing, received forgiveness as a free gift from the one true God, and committed themselves to following Christ's path with the help of the Holy Spirit.

As the translator repeated my words to him, I had time to study the farmer's weatherworn face. He seemed genuinely captivated by the gospel, his brow knit as he intently analyzed each sentence that was interpreted for him. He seemed open and receptive.

The farmer asked some good follow-up questions, which I did my best to answer. He focused on some of the differences between Hinduism and Christianity, particularly the concept of grace, which seemed to fascinate him. He asked me how resurrection was different than reincarnation. It was a stimulating conversation, and I had a welling sense of optimism that he might very well receive Christ right then and there.

But after a while I gradually began to notice a shift. His questions started to stray further and further from the core issues. Soon he was raising halfhearted and rather silly objections to Christianity, as if desperately trying to find some reason *not* to believe in Jesus.

I was puzzled by this change in his demeanor. He was becoming increasingly nervous and agitated. Finally it dawned on me that he might have some subterranean reason to keep Christ at a distance.

"Let me ask this," I said. "Is there something in your life that you're afraid you'll have to give up if you become a follower of Jesus?"

He rocked his head from side to side — a typical mannerism in that part of India — and he began to hem and haw. Then he said something that prompted my translator to say, "Ah, now I understand."

> Soon he was raising halfhearted and rather silly objections to Christianity, as if desperately trying to find some reason *not* to believe in Jesus.

"What is it?" I asked.

"Cockfighting," explained the translator. "He's involved with cockfighting, and he knows he would have to give it up if he were to become a Christian."

At last his smokescreen dissipated and his real reason for resisting God came into the clear. As the translator was giving me this explanation, the farmer looked down at his dusty feet, seemingly ashamed that his secret was out. He shrugged and slowly walked away, brushing off our pleas to continue the conversation.

As he disappeared down the path, I recalled the young ruler in Luke 18 who showed promise when he asked Jesus what he must do to inherit eternal life — but who slouched away, distraught because he couldn't bring himself to pay the price.

Cockfighting was a new one for me; smokescreens are not. While many spiritual seekers have authentic and heartfelt questions about Christianity, some people use objections to fend off faith. They insist that intellectual barriers prevent them from putting their trust in Christ, when in reality there is something in their life that they cherish more than the forgiveness and eternal life offered by Jesus.

I'm not just pointing fingers at others, for this was true about me when I was an atheist. Yes, I had an array of legitimate issues that stood between God and me. And the more I found satisfying answers to those issues, the more I manufactured new objections.

My resistance increased the closer I came toward God and felt the convicting power of the Holy Spirit. Similar to the smokescreen grenades that soldiers detonate in order to hide behind a thick cloud, I would lob irrelevant and half-baked objections in a desperate attempt to obscure the real issue: part of me didn't want to find God because I didn't want to be held accountable for how I was living my life.

My friend Cliffe Knechtle tells the story of meeting a State University of New York student who claimed the Bible was pure mythology, though he had never read it. Knechtle challenged him to read Isaiah, which foretells the Messiah, and Matthew, the gospel that, hundreds of years later, records the fulfillment of those predictions in Jesus.

"It was interesting literature," the student said the next day. "I think it speaks the truth."

When Knechtle asked him if he was ready to put his trust in Christ, however, the student balked. "No way," he insisted. "I have a very active sex life. I know Christ would want to change that. I don't want anyone to change that."

People often have valid questions about Christianity. Other times, however, they raise halfhearted questions in a desperate attempt to block faith.

At least this student was honest about his motives. Usually people aren't so forthright with others or with themselves. They choose instead to use objections as a diversionary tactic to hide their real concern that Jesus simply demands too much.

Action Principle ‹ · · · · · ·

People often have valid questions about Christianity. Other times, however, they raise halfhearted questions in a desperate attempt to block faith. They have hidden motives — most often lifestyle issues — for *not* finding God. One way we can diagnose this smokescreen is to ask, "Is there anything you're afraid you would have to change or give up if you were to become a Christian?"

Stepping into the Adventure ‹ · · · · · ·

Famous atheist Aldous Huxley was up front about his reasons for keeping God at arm's length. As he explained in his book *Ends and Means*:

> I had motives for not wanting the world to have a meaning; consequently assumed that it had none, and was able without any difficulty to find satisfying reasons for this assumption.... For myself, as, no doubt, for most of my contemporaries, the philosophy of meaninglessness was essentially an instrument of liberation. The liberation we desired was simultaneously liberation from a certain political and economic system and liberation from a certain system of morality. We objected to the morality because it interfered with our sexual freedom.[14]

In other words, he was choosing not to believe in God — and finding reasons to justify his skepticism — so that he could continue to pursue an immoral lifestyle.

I wish I could have told Huxley that he was missing the point: God offers *real* liberation. God isn't a curmudgeon who conjures up ways to cramp our style. He loves us and wants to maximize our potential and protect us from behavior he knows is ultimately self-destructive. It was God who created us in the first place; certainly he wants to see us flourish and become all that he intended us to be.

When I encounter people with underlying motivations for avoiding God, hidden or admitted, sometimes I suggest they do a cost/benefit analysis. I urge them to take a piece of paper, divide it down the middle, and compare the benefits and costs of how they're currently living with the pluses and minuses of following Christ.

Think about Christ's side of the ledger. He freely offers forgiveness, a clean conscience, security, guidance, fulfillment, relationships, peace of mind, freedom from guilt and shame, a wholesome moral framework, the promise of eternal life, power over self-destructive tendencies, and the unique hope that comes from being intimately connected with the God of the universe. Oh, and all kinds of exhilarating and unexpected adventures as well.

Then I encourage them to play out the trajectory of their current lifestyle to its logical conclusion. "Where do you end up?" I ask. "How will you cope with the tragedies you're going to encounter along the way? How will you feel about yourself? And what will you draw hope from in the end?"

I tell them about my own experiences. Ever since I said to God, "Take my life," I've been on a white-knuckle adventure that blows the doors off of how I used to get my kicks. "But go ahead," I tell them. "Play it out for yourself on paper."

This kind of a challenge can be useful in helping them see past their diversionary tactics and start seriously considering the benefits of a life — and an eternity — united with Christ.

Inspiration for the Journey ‹ · · · · ·

For whoever wants to save his life will lose it, but whoever loses his life for me will save it.

Jesus in Luke 9:24

POTENTIAL IN PARTNERING

MARK MITTELBERG

It was a conversation I wouldn't have gotten into on my own. In fact, I'll admit that I barely noticed the guy behind the counter as I breezed into the ice-cream shop that evening. I quickly headed to the far end of the shop, and about the time I read that the flavor of the day was White Chocolate Mousse, I heard my friend Karl ask the man the question.

Karl is a straight-shooting, hard-hitting type-A entrepreneur who buys and sells businesses as easily as most of us change socks. He is highly successful and accustomed to being in charge. He also passionately loves God and people, and he is constantly looking for ways to introduce them to each other.

Karl is also a classic example of the "Direct Style" of evangelism that we teach as one of six biblical approaches in the *Becoming a Contagious Christian* book and training course. He doesn't like small talk, preferring instead to get right to the point. He enjoys stirring up action, whether participating in corporate board meetings, making business deals, offering ideas at ministry

> It was a conversation I wouldn't have gotten into on my own.

planning retreats, or — like right then — striking up a conversation with the guy behind an ice-cream counter.

"Based on your appearance and accent," I heard Karl say to the man after exchanging initial hellos, "I'm guessing you're from somewhere in the Middle East ..."

That caught my attention, but what Karl said next surprised me as much as it seemed to surprise the fellow he was talking to. "... so that makes me curious: are you a Muslim or a Christian?"

About then I started thinking Rocky Road might be a more appropriate ice cream of the day. But before I could get too concerned about how the guy might react, he answered.

"That's an interesting question. I grew up in a Muslim country and was raised in the Islamic faith. But I've been here in America for a couple of years now, and I've met some really great Christians. I don't know what to think. I guess, to be honest with you, I'm somewhere in the middle right now, trying to figure out what to believe."

Gulp. Forget the ice cream.

With characteristic command, Karl said, "That's fascinating," and quickly got the guy's name, then he motioned for me to come closer. Karl knew that my preferred approach to evangelism is the "Intellectual Style," which is another of the six styles we teach in the *Contagious* course.

"Mark, I'd like you to meet my new friend, Fayz. And Fayz, this is Mark; he likes to study and talk about these kinds of topics."

As the two of us shook hands, Karl turned to me and added, "Fayz wants to know more about Jesus and why we trust in him instead of in Muhammad." *He does?* I thought to myself, probably just as Fayz thought to himself, *I do?*

"All right," I said, scrambling to think of what I could say to succinctly explain the important differences to him. Soon after I started my explanation, somebody else came into the shop to order a sundae. As people came and went from the shop, I did my best to explain who Jesus really is, but the traffic in and out became increasingly distracting.

"I'll tell you what, Fayz," I said, "it's hard to go much deeper right now, but a friend of mine, Lee Strobel, wrote a book that relates to this, called *The Case for Christ*. If you'd be willing to take a look at it, I'll bring you a copy."

He politely agreed, seeming relieved that we weren't going to try to continue the conversation right then. So we bought our ice cream, found out when it would work for us to come back, and left.

A couple of days later we brought a copy of Lee's book to Fayz and again encouraged him to read it. Shortly after that I flew home to Chicago.

However, Karl didn't let my leaving slow him down. He brought his wife, Barbara, into the shop to meet Fayz. She is a great example of what we refer to in the *Contagious* training as the "Interpersonal Style," which means she's adept at sharing Christ through relationships. She naturally befriended him and found out about his wife and their little girl. Before long, the couples were inviting each other into their homes for meals, and Karl urged Fayz and his family to visit their church as well.

It didn't stop there. Karl and Barbara were part of a large adult class at their church, and they told the group about how they were reaching out to Fayz and his wife. They asked for prayer and challenged their friends to do some evangelistic ice-cream outings themselves—a dangerous proposition to make to a bunch of hungry Baptists.

Before long there were many more Christians meeting Fayz, building friendships with him and his wife, inviting them to various events, sharing their testimonies, and answering spiritual questions. When the group discovered that Fayz was a medical student who was selling ice cream to pay his way through school, some of them served him by helping him make connections with the local medical community. In short, all six of the styles of evangelism that we teach in the *Contagious* course — direct, testimonial, intellectual, interpersonal, serving, and invitational — were being deployed by a band of believers who were partnering powerfully in their outreach efforts.

Along the way, something amazing was happening. Fayz started opening up to Jesus. Finally, almost a year after that original conversation, Fayz, his wife, and their six-year-old daughter all committed their lives to Christ at a service at Karl and Barbara's church.

Since that time, Fayz has graduated from medical school, become a doctor, and relocated to another part of the country. We've kept in touch with him, helping him and his family get involved in a church near their new home. Fayz has continued to grow in his relationship with Christ, and he even joined me on stage at a pastor's conference to tell his story of becoming a follower of Jesus through the collective efforts of Karl, Barbara, me, and many others.

It truly was a team effort: a variety of Christians with very different personalities and approaches, all cooperating with each other and with the Holy Spirit to reach out to a Muslim man and his family who matter so much to God.

> Action Principle

Two of the greatest impediments to diving into the adventure of evangelism are believing you have to be like someone else and thinking you have to do everything on your own. Neither is true. You can be yourself, using the unique style and personality God gave you. And you can partner with other Christians in your church or small group, praying and working together to try to more effectively reach all of your family members and friends for Christ.

Stepping into the Adventure ◀ · · · · ·

Jesus said that he came "to seek and to save what was lost" (Luke 19:10), but he also involved twelve partners in his ministry efforts. And when he sent out a team of seventy-two to spread his message, he instructed them to go in groups of two (Luke 10:1).

There really is strength in numbers, and when it comes to spreading our faith, that's all the more true when we each identify and build upon our own special styles of evangelism. Karl is like Peter in Acts 2: bold and direct. I'm more like Paul in Acts 17, using reason and logic to present the faith. Barbara is similar to Matthew who, according to Luke 5:29 (where it refers to him as Levi), held a big party as a way to deepen his relationships with his former coworkers. Lee, whose book we gave to Fayz, combines the story-based testimonial style, like the blind man healed by Jesus in John 9, with intellectual answers.

> There really is strength in numbers.

Others from Karl and Barbara's class are more invitational, like the Samaritan woman in John 4, and service-oriented, like Tabitha, who made clothing for needy people in Acts 9. The combination of all these approaches, working in partnership, was powerful in God's hands — and in the lives of Fayz and his family.

So how can you apply the principles in this story to your own life? Consider which of these six biblical styles — or combination of styles — best fits you. Experiment with several to discover which are most natural to your God-given personality. For more information on these styles, read the *Becoming a Contagious Christian* book or, better yet, take your class or small group through the updated training course (see Recommended Resources for more information; the curriculum is now on DVD so Lee and I can come to your group and teach it for you).

As you discover your own evangelism style as well as the styles of others in your church or fellowship, you'll be able to intentionally partner with those whose approaches best supplement yours — and fit the needs of the people you're trying to reach. Together, as a team, you'll experience the thrill of impacting others for Christ.

> Inspiration for the Journey

Two are better than one, because they have a good return for their work: If one falls down, his friend can help him up.

Ecclesiastes 4:9 – 10

IN THE NICK OF TIME

LEE STROBEL

I'll confess that I was always a little afraid of Leslie's father. Al was the rough-hewn product of Cicero, Illinois (Al Capone's old stomping grounds, he would remind me), a stout, brusque, and fiercely opinionated barber who found his niche later in life shearing off soldiers' hair at a military base. When you got through his tough-as-nails exterior, however, you'd find a heart of gold — but it wasn't always easy to bore through.

Still, we did enjoy one thing in common: we were both satisfied atheists. That is until Leslie became a follower of Jesus, and then, two years later, I did as well. One of the first things I said to Leslie after I became a Christian was, "We should tell Al about this."

The very next time we got together, in a burst of naive enthusiasm, I excitedly told Al the story of my spiritual journey. My unstated implication was, *Hey, Al, you should become a Christian too.*

Al's expression remained stoic. "Look, that's fine for you," he said, jabbing a finger at me to punctuate his point, "but don't ever bring up Jesus to me again, okay?"

To his credit, through the following years Al never criticized or tried to impede or inhibit my faith in any way. In fact, when I later told him with great trepidation that I was going to leave my newspaper career and take a 60 percent pay cut to work at a church, he surprised me by being supportive. "If that's what you feel you want to do with your life," he said, "then you should do it."

For the next twenty years, all Leslie and I could do for Al was to authentically live out our faith and to pray for him consistently. Yet through it all, we saw not one glimmer of interest in spiritual matters. His language remained just as coarse, his skepticism toward church never softened, and he stayed steadfastly indifferent toward God.

Then one day Al suffered a stroke. Leslie and I huddled with his doctor at the nurse's station outside Al's hospital room. After going through an elaborate medical explanation that neither of us quite understood, the doctor gave this ominous prognosis: "Al is going to have a series of these strokes over the next several months until one of them is fatal."

When Al was released from the hospital, Leslie and I moved him and his wife, Helen, who was a Christian, to a house close to ours. Al's mind was sharp, but he became increasingly lethargic. We avoided the uncomfortable topic of his diagnosis, never coming out and explicitly discussing his condition with him. It was simply understood that Al was slowly fading away.

Finally, I couldn't take it anymore. My usual evangelistic style is testimonial; in other words, I tend to tell the story of my journey to faith as a way of engaging spiritually curious people. I also use an intellectual approach, discussing questions or objections with seekers over time. Other Christians tend to be more direct in their evangelistic efforts, in fitting with their personality. As for me, I'm generally uncomfortable with personal confrontations and try to avoid them whenever I can.

But in the case of my father-in-law, I couldn't avoid it any longer. One day I encouraged Leslie and Helen to go out shopping so Al and I could be alone. After they left I pulled up a chair to face Al, who was seated in a recliner in his living room.

"Al," I said with intensity, "do you realize you're dying? Do you understand that you don't have much longer in this world?"

Al looked at me with sadness in his eyes, but he didn't say anything.

"I don't want to be in heaven without you. Leslie and Helen and the grandkids — none of us wants to be in heaven without you. *Please*, Al," I pleaded.

Still, there was no response. He stared straight ahead, his arms crossed. He sat very, very still.

"Al, you can be in heaven with all of us. Jesus paid the price for your sins. If you admit your wrongdoing — and, Al, you know you haven't always lived the way you should — then you can receive Christ's forgiveness for everything you've ever done wrong. He will wipe your slate clean and open the door to heaven for you. It's a free gift, Al. Why wouldn't you want to receive it?"

I could tell Al was tracking my every word, but he remained silent. I didn't know what else to say — and that's when I did something I had never done before, but which seemed so very necessary at the moment.

I sat back in my chair and whispered under my breath so that Al, who was hard of hearing, couldn't make out what I was saying: "Satan, unhand him! Let him go! He is *not* yours!" I felt like the Evil One actually had him in his grasp and was going to drag him away.

I turned back to Al and continued to implore him to receive Jesus. I explained repentance as best I could. I emphasized that

> I didn't know what else to say — and that's when I did something I had never done before.

despite his best intentions to live a good life, he was a sinner who needed God's grace. And slowly I began to see a crack in Al's facade. Something in his face told me his heart was opening.

"Al, you want to confess your sins and receive Christ right now, don't you?" I asked. Then I held my breath.

Instantly, tears filled his eyes and Al slowly nodded. I breathed a sigh of relief, then led him, sentence by sentence, through a simple prayer of repentance and faith. The whole time, my heart felt like it was going to explode.

At the end, a smile played at the corner of Al's mouth. I went over and hugged him like never before. "Welcome home, Al!" I declared. "Welcome home!"

Almost on cue, Leslie and Helen returned from shopping, and I told them the news. They erupted in celebration, and Al beamed as they hugged and kissed him.

This was time for a party! Leslie started to cook a special dinner, but after a little while we noticed that something was wrong with Al. His right side was suddenly weak.

"He's having another stroke!" Leslie screamed.

We called 911, and when the paramedics arrived, they quickly loaded him into the ambulance. Leslie climbed inside. I drove with Helen in our car to the hospital. The ambulance arrived first. As they began wheeling Al into the emergency room, he looked up at Leslie and said softly, "Tell Lee thanks."

It turned out that this stroke was the one that would destroy Al's mind. He was left in a state of constant confusion. Al ended up lingering for several weeks, and then he finally went Home.

So in the last cogent conversation of his life, after more than eight decades of ardent atheism, Al Hirdler — one of the last persons I ever thought would receive Jesus — finally opened his heart to God's outrageous gift of grace.

Just in the nick of time.

Action Principle

All of us have a style of evangelism that syncs up well with our personality, yet there are circumstances where we need to move beyond our usual approach in order to reach someone who's in urgent need of Christ. Yes, it may make us feel a bit awkward, *but our discomfort isn't nearly as important as their eternity.*

> Our discomfort isn't nearly as important as their eternity.

Stepping into the Adventure

Sometimes we have no choice; we *have* to act—and fast. I remember when Mark Mittelberg and I were in the church basement and he got a large pill caught in his windpipe. His airflow blocked, he looked at me in wide-eyed panic.

I had no experience with medical emergencies. I had never taken a first aid course. I could have dialed 911, but he would have suffocated before the paramedics got there. So I performed the Heimlich maneuver on Mark and, fortunately, it worked on the second try—just in the nick of time.

Another time, when I was fourteen years old, I became trapped in a fire in the basement of our family's suburban Chicago home. A police officer arrived before the firefighters, and that policeman knew he had to act immediately. So without the specialized training of the firefighters, he entered the fiery, smoke-filled basement and led me to safety—just in the nick of time.

There are instances when God might use you to rescue someone from an even worse fate. You may know a person with only a short time to live, or one departing on a dangerous mission that could jeopardize her safety, or someone you will probably never get a chance to see again, someone without other Christian influences in his life. At such times, merely planting a spiritual seed isn't enough. We have to cast aside our own discomfort and adopt some of the apostle Peter's direct or confrontational style, even though it may not be our own.

But have confidence: when those circumstances arise, you won't be alone. As I found while I was desperately trying to rescue Al from an eternity apart from God, there was Someone who loved him even more than I did. The Holy Spirit showed up to thwart Satan and drive my otherwise ineffective words deep into Al's heart — just in the nick of time.

You can trust that when you've pushed yourself as far as you can in the adventure of evangelism, at that critical time, he is going to show up for you too.

> Inspiration for the Journey

See to it that no one misses the grace of God.

Hebrews 12:15

MAKING ROOM FOR QUESTIONS

MARK MITTELBERG

"I used to be a Christian."

Those were the first words out of the young man's mouth. We'd never met before, but he had called because someone told him I would take his spiritual questions seriously. His opening line grabbed my full attention. As our telephone conversation went on, I soon realized that I was his final recourse in a last-ditch effort to get some answers before permanently abandoning his faith.

"Look, these issues you're raising are serious. I don't want to offer quick-fix answers over the phone," I told him. "How about coming to my office so we can sit down and really work through some of your questions?"

He seemed surprised. "You'd be willing to do that?"

"Of course I would. When can you come in?" I replied, surprised that he was surprised by my willingness to meet when so much was at stake. We lined up an appointment, and when the time came, he arrived with a friend who, I quickly found out, had many of the same spiritual roadblocks.

As their story unfolded, I learned that they had been part of a nearby congregation that was fairly authoritarian in its approach. The church declared the truth and expected its members to accept it — no questions asked. The problem was that my two high school friends *did* have questions, and they kept asking them.

The first time they raised their objections during a class at church, their teacher shut them down. "Those are things that people of faith must accept *by faith*," he insisted. "You just need to believe, and then you'll know that it's true."

> My two high school friends *did* have questions, and they kept asking them.

To my friends — as well as to me — this sounded like an admission that there are no good reasons to believe, so you just have to accept it as part of a blind leap in the dark. Kind of like saying, "Leap before you look; you might get lucky."

When I asked how they handled that encounter, they told me they tried to comply, but their doubts only grew. Later that summer they had gone to their church camp, where they had a different set of leaders. They decided to give it another try, but once again the people in charge silenced them. "You must not raise these issues here," they warned. "You'll only confuse the other campers."

So they held in their questions while their doubts continued to fester, poisoning their faith.

"Then what did you do?" I asked, trying not to let out my real feelings about how they had been so horribly mishandled.

"Well, we finally decided that the Bible couldn't be trusted and that the Christian faith teaches things it can't prove. So we basically abandoned our belief in God," they said.

As disturbing as that was, what I heard next just about knocked me out of my chair.

"And this fall we changed what had been our weekly Bible

study into a 'Skeptics Group.' It's a place where we invite our friends from school to come hear the evidence *against* the Bible and Christianity."

"That's ... fascinating," I said, trying to stay calm. "So what made you come and tell me all of this?"

"A friend challenged us, saying that before we go any further we ought to slow down and test our thinking one more time. He gave us your name and said you might be able to help us out."

"Well, I'm really glad you're here, and I'm willing to do whatever it takes to help you get answers to your objections," I said, hoping to encourage them with good information as well as my personal interest. "I also want to tell you up front that I'm confident in the truth of Christianity and anxious to discuss whatever has been hurting your faith."

With that, we launched into a three-hour conversation about their main areas of concern, which included many of the standard objections about why God allows evil and suffering, questions about the reliability of the Bible, and problems with hypocrisy among religious people — both past and present. By no means easy issues, but certainly not new ones either.

By the end of that discussion, I could tell that their doubts were beginning to dissolve. But what came next got me even more excited.

"Before we go, can I make a request?"

"Sure. What is it?"

"I was wondering if you'd be willing to come to our next Skeptics Group meeting at my house to explain some of this information to the rest of our friends. I think they'd be interested in what you have to say."

"Yes," I said, not needing more than a nanosecond to think about it. "When do you meet?" He gave me the details, and then I asked him one more question: "When I invited you to meet with me today, you brought a friend with you, which is great. Now you're inviting me to come and meet with you; would it be okay if I bring a friend with me?"

"Of course," he answered.

We said good-bye until the next time we would see each other at the upcoming Skeptics Group.

The following week I went to his house, bringing with me Lee "*The Case for Christ*" Strobel. We had a grand time talking for hours with this circle of sincere but spiritually confused teenagers, sharing our testimonies, answering their questions, and challenging their thinking.

God really worked during our time together, so much so that by the end of the evening the original student had recommitted his life to Christ. And within two weeks the friend he had brought to my office became a believer.

Then together they converted their Skeptics Group back into a bona fide Bible study and started reaching out to their friends at school, showing them the truths that support their faith and encouraging them to follow Jesus, just as they were now doing.

All because someone was willing to make room for questions.

> Action Principle

When someone harbors doubts about faith, it doesn't help to tell them they simply must try harder to believe. Spiritual confidence — our own and that of the people we want to reach — comes when we ask questions honestly, face objections squarely, and present information accurately. Ultimately, our faith is not true because we believe it; rather, we believe it because it is true. Christians, and every-

> Our faith is not true because we believe it; rather, we believe it because it is true.

one searching for God, should be lovers of truth who base their beliefs on what is real. We have nothing to fear because our faith rests on a bedrock of genuine facts.

Stepping into the Adventure

It's easy to say that our faith is built on facts, but it's another to really *believe* it. We can't convey spiritual confidence to others if we don't possess it ourselves. So what can we do to gain assurance of our beliefs?

There's no way around it: you've *gotta* do your homework. Think of the last time you took a major test. It didn't help to know that your instructor understood the information or that the student next to you could ace the exam. The only way you could go in with confidence was for you to do the hard work of learning and reviewing the information until you knew for certain that you really knew it. Self-assurance doesn't come vicariously from others or through intellectual osmosis. You've got to get it the old fashioned way: through serious study.

Likewise, you aren't going to be sure of your beliefs just because your pastor, teacher, or small group leader is sure of his or hers. Yes, their confidence can bolster yours but only temporarily while you strive to learn what they've already discovered. And the only way to learn that is by doing some faith-oriented homework.

The apostle Paul said, "Do your best to present yourself to God as one approved, a workman who does not need to be ashamed and who correctly handles the word of truth" (2 Timothy 2:15). This includes spending time reading, studying, and even memorizing parts of the Bible. There is no substitute for knowing the Word of God so you can accurately and convincingly convey God's truths to people you talk to.

Still, that's not enough in a secular culture like ours. Today if you answer someone's question by quoting a Bible verse, you'll likely be asked why you believe the Bible. When that happens, it won't be enough to sing the Sunday school song, "The B-I-B-L-E, yes, that's the book for me!" You'll need to know *why* it's the book for you rather than some other religious text — or none at all.

That information can be gained by reading books such as *The Case for Christ* and *The Case for Faith* as well as my *Choosing Your Faith ... In a World of Spiritual Options*, which shows the best criteria for selecting what to believe and presents twenty arguments for choosing Christianity.

Reading these books and studying Scripture will go a long way toward expanding your spiritual confidence and preparing you to answer the questions from the next skeptical high school student or curious neighbor you happen to encounter.

> Inspiration for the Journey

But in your hearts set apart Christ as Lord. Always be prepared to give an answer to everyone who asks you to give the reason for the hope that you have. But do this with gentleness and respect.

1 Peter 3:15

THE BIG OOPS

LEE STROBEL

I was feeling euphoric because a conference that Mark and I had staged in a southern city went much better than we had anticipated. The morning after the event, we decided to walk over to a restaurant adjacent to our hotel and have a celebratory breakfast before flying back to California.

The eatery had a large wooden porch and a row of rocking chairs where visitors could relax and people watch. In one chair was a woman about eighteen years old with dark hair and dark eyes, and sitting next to her was a young man about the same age.

We had to walk past them to get to the door, and just as we were stepping in front of the young woman, I heard her say, "What's a deist?"

> Just as we were stepping in front of the young woman, I heard her say, "What's a deist?"

I couldn't believe it; I had just written a book that dealt with that topic. I instantly turned on my heels and came face-to-face with the teenager.

"A deist is somebody who believes that God created the universe and then he walked away," I declared, rattling off material from my recent research and writings. "A deist believes that God wound up the universe like a giant clock and is merely letting it tick down. A deist believes that God is distant, detached, and disinterested. *But*," I emphasized, "that's *not* what the evidence shows."

By this point I was really getting revved up. I was so excited to find a young person who actually cared about these important matters. Barely pausing to catch my breath, I unleashed a series of facts that demonstrated God's continual involvement in the cosmos well after the initial moment of creation.

I talked about cosmology, physics, and astronomy, pointing out how the incredible fine-tuning of the universe and the intricate functioning of our planet continue to this day in ways that defy a naturalistic explanation.

Her eyes got wide.

Without missing a beat, I launched into a soliloquy about the biological evidence for the creation of life, describing how God must have been involved in the design of the first living cell at some point after the universe came into existence.

Her eyes got wider.

Shifting without the clutch, I immediately went into a discussion of history, pointing out that God most emphatically proved his ongoing concern for humankind by sending his Son into the world in order to open up the way to heaven for us.

She stared at me, her mouth open.

I segued into a staccato-like recitation of the evidence for the resurrection of Jesus — including early reports that cannot be legendary, a tomb that even his critics conceded was empty, and eyewitness accounts — to drive home the point that because Jesus returned from the dead, his followers will someday too.

She didn't utter a word.

Not stopping there, I stressed that Mark and I were among

millions of people around the world and throughout history who have personally felt God's presence, guidance, encouragement, and even his stunning answers to prayers that can only be described as miraculous. Surely, I said, this shows his continuing love and interaction with his followers.

I knew that in my exuberance I had gone on far too long without even giving this young woman a chance to say anything or ask a question. Honestly, I've never gotten that carried away before or since. I was so giddy over the success of our conference and so thrilled to have someone ask a question I was prepped to answer that I simply couldn't contain myself.

Finally, I turned to Mark and said, "Can you believe it? We just happened to be walking past her and she said, 'What's a deist?'"

Mark had a pained look on his face. "Uh, Lee," he replied hesitantly, "I think what she said was, *'Buenos dias.'*"

Uh-oh. Now *my* eyes got wide. Utterly embarrassed — and for the first time, completely speechless — I glanced back at her and then at her boyfriend. And at that moment, all four of us burst into laughter.

"Oops" was all I could sputter as we howled together.

Without a doubt, it was an embarrassing moment. Fortunately, that wasn't the end of our encounter. After all, the ice had been broken. How could we *not* have a spiritual conversation at that point? As humiliating as that experience was for me, it didn't bother the young woman or her friend at all. On the contrary, they were anxious to talk about God.

It turned out the young man was a high school senior who was in town for a big track meet, and his companion was his girlfriend who had come along to cheer him on. We introduced ourselves — trying to establish that we were, in fact, *normal* — and began talking about how a person can know God.

After a while, the girl said, "Why don't you come meet the rest of the team? I think they'd be interested in this."

We agreed, and the two of them brought us back to their meeting room at the adjacent hotel, where we found the coach and several other athletes resting before their competition. When we told them how we had met their two friends, they had a good laugh too. And then some of them began to ask questions about Christianity.

In the end, we talked for roughly half an hour about various spiritual matters. What had started out as a big faux pas emerged as a great opportunity to talk about God with people we otherwise would never have met.

> What had started out as a big faux pas emerged as a great opportunity to talk about God with people we otherwise would never have met.

There's something refreshing about laughter. If that young man and woman had responded angrily to my over-the-top monologue, or if I had slunk away in embarrassment rather than laugh at myself, that would have been the end of any opportunity to interact on a meaningful level. I was grateful that instead we all enjoyed a moment of levity and then were able to use it as a starting point to delve into deeper topics.

Comedian and musician Victor Borge was right. "Laughter," he observed, "is the shortest distance between two people."

> Action Principle

Lighten up. Although we have a serious and even convicting message, we don't have to take ourselves too seriously. Humor can lubricate conversations, forge an instant bond between strangers, and quickly create rapport where none had existed — even when the joke is on us.

Stepping into the Adventure ⟨ · · · · ·

As Sheldon Vanauken famously noted, when Christians are "somber and joyless, when they are self-righteous and smug in complacent consecration, when they are narrow and repressive, then Christianity dies a thousand deaths."[15]

Well, we don't have to be that way. In fact, we *shouldn't* be.

If anyone should be joyful and optimistic, full of life and enthusiasm, it's people whose guilt has been permanently lifted off their shoulders, who have a personal relationship with their Creator, and who are assured of spending eternity in his perfect presence. What's not to like about all that? We ought to be ready to laugh, quick with a winsome quip, and eager to see the lighter side of life.

Humor is important in the adventure of personal evangelism because it dismantles stereotypes about Christians, it shows we're ordinary and enjoy having a good time (the kind of good times that don't bring regret), and it establishes common ground. In other words, we usually laugh because we can personally identify with the situation being presented.

What's more, humor breaks down defenses. For years I had heard the psychological principle that people are more receptive to new ideas when they're laughing, but I saw it for myself when I was watching a TV show. Though the program was endorsing behavior that I didn't agree with, the humor had me laughing so hard that I was actually feeling positive toward what was being promoted.

Finally I had to stop myself. *Wait a second; this is just propaganda. I don't believe this stuff.* My laughter had diminished my defenses to the point where ideas I didn't agree with were starting to gain a foothold.

Of course, that doesn't mean we should cynically inject calculated humor to gain a psychological advantage. But it does illustrate the power of laughter as an essential element in human interaction. There's no need for us to be a curmudgeon like the one portrayed by W. C. Fields, whose philosophy was "smile first thing in the morning and get it over with."

No, the apostle Paul urges us to have a different outlook. Despite suffering terrible deprivation, beatings, shipwrecks, and imprisonment, he encouraged us to "be joyful always" (1 Thessalonians 5:16). That's good advice, especially when we're trying to help seekers understand that the Christian life isn't just the only way to die — it's also the best way to live.

❯ Inspiration for the Journey

[There is] a time to weep and a time to laugh, a time to mourn and a time to dance.

Ecclesiastes 3:4

THE IMPACT
OF EVIDENCE

MARK MITTELBERG

"I'd *like* to become a Christian, but I still have a few questions that are hanging me up," said John Swift, a fast-talking, hard-hitting commercial banker who worked in downtown Chicago.

I was meeting with him for the first time at the request of Ernie, a leader of one of our small groups for seekers at our church, who had been dealing for some time with John's list of spiritual doubts and objections. "Let's talk about whatever is holding you back," I told John. "I hope you know you don't need to have an answer to every question in order to become a Christian."

> "I'd *like* to become a Christian, but I still have a few questions that are hanging me up," said John Swift.

"I realize that," he replied. "But if I'm reading you guys right, my main question deals with something you all consider to be a fairly big deal."

"Maybe or maybe not," I said. "What is it?"

Emphatically, John shot back, "I don't believe in the resurrection of Christ."

At this point I had to concede that, yes, that issue *is* a big deal to us in the church. "I'll admit that when I went to seminary, the resurrection of Christ fell under the heading of *biggies*. That's because the Bible clearly teaches that this is one of the truths essential to being a follower of Christ. But I'm curious, why don't you believe Jesus rose from the dead?"

"It just doesn't make sense to me that a dead person could come back to life," he explained. "Everything I've ever seen supports the fact that dead people simply stay in the grave and their bodies rot there or get eaten by wild dogs. Why should I believe it was any different for Jesus?"

It was a great question. Why should we put our faith in a claim that contradicts everything we've ever seen or experienced? Before venturing a response, I decided to ask him what he'd been doing to study the matter.

"Mostly," he replied, "I've just read and listened to the scholars featured in the media."

"Which ones?" I asked, fearing the very response I was about to hear.

"I don't know all of their names," John replied, "but they're part of something called the Jesus Seminar, and I've got to tell you that those guys have all kinds of negative things to say about the idea of Jesus rising from the dead."

"I'm very aware of that," I said, sounding a bit more impatient than I'd intended. "Haven't you read any of the great books that present the actual historical evidence for the resurrection, such as the writings of Norman Geisler, Josh McDowell, or Gary Habermas?"

"Honestly, Mark, I don't know about any of their books, and I've never really heard anything that sounded like genuine evidence for Jesus' resurrection. Maybe you can fill me in."

"I'd be happy to," I replied, as we launched into an hour-plus discussion about some of the key points of evidence. The more we talked, the more encouraged I was by John's receptivity. At the same time, I was amazed and frustrated that so many spiritually inquisitive seekers are completely unaware of such vitally important information, even though it has been around for two thousand years.

The minutes flew by, and soon we were out of time. "Before you go," I said to John, "I'd like to loan you a book that I think will help deepen your understanding of the overwhelming amount of evidence that supports the resurrection."

Handing him my copy of *Jesus Under Fire*, edited by Michael Wilkins and J. P. Moreland, I added, "I'm sure the whole book would be helpful to you, but I'd especially like to encourage you to read through the chapter titled 'Did Jesus Rise from the Dead?' by William Lane Craig. I think it will clearly address your question."[16]

Then I added one more thought that even surprised me. "John, I know you're a businessman who relates to challenges and goals. So let me urge you to read that chapter right away and maybe look at some of the other books I've been telling you about so you can see how strong the evidence really is. Then, assuming you confirm this to be true, I want to challenge you to become a Christian before Easter, which is only about a month away. That way you'll be able to finally celebrate the holiday for its real meaning."

The look of intensity in John's eyes told me he was taking my challenge seriously. It wasn't more than a couple of weeks later that he sent my book back with a note informing me that he'd already combed through the chapter by Bill Craig several times, read the entire book, and then went out and purchased several copies of the book for himself and a few friends who were asking similar questions. (I love it when *non-Christians* get involved in the adventure of evangelism.)

About two weeks later, while I was on a speaking trip in Australia, I phoned in to listen to my voicemails, and I heard a message that took my breath away. Ernie, John's seeker small group leader, excitedly reported that John had trusted in Christ *just a few days before Easter*. When I got back home, I called John to congratulate and encourage him. Soon after, I had the privilege of baptizing him in the pond by our church.

For me, this was another vivid illustration of how God uses answers to tough questions to clear away obstacles and open a person's heart for the gospel. Through the years, I've lost count of the number of times that I've seen the Holy Spirit perform this kind of spiritual jujitsu, employing logic and evidence to turn an objection to Christianity into another reason to believe.

> Action Principle

Many people, probably some of your own family and friends, are just a few good answers away from taking Christ seriously. Yes, other concerns will sometimes arise, including lifestyle issues and a lack of willingness to yield their lives to God. But as long as people are held back by intellectual objections, they will use those as reasons for not considering changes in those other areas of their lives. So we must be ready to wield logic and evidence in order to show that the Christian faith is true and worth fully embracing.

> We must be ready to wield logic and evidence in order to show that the Christian faith is true and worth fully embracing.

Stepping into the Adventure ◄ · · · · ·

Would you know what to say to a friend who challenged you with a question like the one John asked me? Unfortunately, many Christians respond by saying, "Well, you've got to take it on faith." Or "The Bible says it's true and that settles it." Some might even assume the person must be destined for God's judgment and unable to see the truth, so why even try?

The Bible tells us we should be ready to give a clear and thoughtful response. First Peter 3:15 says, "Always be prepared to give an answer to everyone who asks you to give the reason for the hope that you have. But do this with gentleness and respect." The Greek word that is translated "answer" in that verse is *apologia*, which means "a speech of defense." It's from this that we get our term *apologetics*, which is a reasoned defense of our faith.

It's important to know that this directive is not just for pastors, professors, and theologians. The verse tells *all of us* as followers of Christ to be ready to explain and support our faith. Consequently, it's imperative that we read good books, sign up for appropriate classes and seminars, listen to trustworthy teaching CDs and radio programs, take notes at church, and do whatever "homework" is necessary to become well versed in the information that backs up our beliefs.

But none of us ever feels completely up to the task. Even when we do have a good response, the situation isn't always conducive to giving it. That's why you'll notice that in a number of these accounts, including this one, Lee and I recommend a book that we're confident will help answer the person's questions. We do this because we've seen time and again how the combination of personal conversations and credible printed resources can move people, like John, beyond their intellectual roadblocks to the point of trusting in Christ.

In order to know what books to give people, you first need to read the books, and to be able to actually provide someone with a copy, you need to invest in extras to have on hand (see Recommended Resources for a list of suggestions). Personally, I find that when I have copies available, especially when I'm traveling, I'm more apt to get into spiritual conversations. That's because I know I don't need to answer every question; I've got backup.

So how can you step into the adventure of giving good answers and evidence to help people in their spiritual journeys? Read, listen, study, prepare, and invest in resources that can equip you and assist your friend in taking steps toward Christ.

⟫ Inspiration for the Journey

The weapons we fight with are not the weapons of the world. On the contrary, they have divine power to demolish strongholds. We demolish arguments and every pretension that sets itself up against the knowledge of God, and we take captive every thought to make it obedient to Christ.

2 Corinthians 10:4 – 5

ORDINARY LIFE, EXTRAORDINARY IMPACT

LEE STROBEL

Bill McMillen didn't have a degree in theology. He didn't work on the staff of a church. He was a bespectacled, average-looking, moderately successful financial consultant with a busy life and lots of commitments.

But as someone who was rescued by Jesus from a pretty wild life in 1982, Bill was committed to bringing Christ's message of hope and redemption to as many people as he could. As much as anyone I know, he lived a life of maximum impact.

Mark and I were friends with Bill, and when we attended his funeral after he died a few years ago, the church did something unusual at the ceremony: microphones were set up so anyone could tell a personal story about Bill. As we listened in astonishment, person after person stepped up to tell how God used this ordinary businessman to have an extraordinary influence in their life.

> Person after person stepped up to tell how God used this ordinary businessman to have an extraordinary influence in their life.

One of Bill's childhood friends named John described how he had gone through a midlife crisis, gotten a divorce, and moved back to the Chicago area. "That's when Bill got hold of me and he wouldn't let me go," John said. People nodded, knowing Bill's reputation for tenacity.

Every Saturday night, Bill would pick up John and bring him to church to hear the gospel. He invited John into a Bible study to learn more about God. He'd call him on the phone and talk to him over coffee. It wasn't long before John committed his life to Christ. Then, in rapid succession, so did his teenage son and daughter.

Choking back tears, John described how the three of them were baptized together in a pond outside his church. "All of this came about," he said, "because Bill McMillen was faithful and true to Christ Jesus."

Then a woman named Maggie told about how she had been going through tough financial times and made an appointment to consult with Bill. When he came out to greet her in his waiting room, she was perusing the Christian literature that he always kept there.

"Are you a Christian?" Bill asked.

"Well, not really," she said.

"Look, let's talk about your finances later. Let's talk about God first. What do you think about God right now?"

Her eyebrows shot up. "Ooookay ..."

He gave her a Bible and showed her how to study it. He drew illustrations to make the gospel understandable. A short time later, she received Christ and soon became a key volunteer at Bill's highly evangelistic church.

A lawyer named Jim talked about how his life had been collapsing around him. He told Bill, "I've got to get out of town, out of my marriage, out of my profession, maybe out of my life."

Bill suggested they take a trip together. "Okay," said Jim, "I've got a van."

"Does it have a tape player?" Bill asked.

"No," said Jim. "It's my fishing van. It's a rickety old thing."

Bill showed up for the trip lugging two cassette tape players and thirty-seven Christian teaching tapes. "I remember it was thirty-seven because Bill wouldn't let me out of the van until we had listened to every single one of them," Jim recalled with a chuckle. Then he added, in a voice now cracking with emotion, "And that is how I came to Christ, and my life was changed forever."

A businessman stood to say he had met Bill when his company was embroiled in financial turmoil and sought Bill's advice. "At four o'clock, Bill showed up with a yellow legal pad and a pencil and started firing away with questions," he said. "By five o'clock, he had saved my business — and I found myself signed up for a Monday morning Bible study in his office. And before long, I was saved by Jesus."

A guy named Lou said he too had turned to Bill due to financial woes. "But Bill's agenda was totally different," he said. "He put his life on hold for four or five days and became more than a business consultant; he became a minister. We got in the car and drove to Arizona and spent a lot of time wandering in the desert, looking for offbeat hamburger places to try. During the course of that time, there were Christian books and tapes and Bible passages and constant talk about Jesus. It was during that trip that I committed myself to Christ."

Bill's business partner spoke next. "Bill was a man who never had any good intentions about what he was going to do in the future," he said. "Bill did everything right then and there. The time to act was now. If someone's in need, help him or her — *now*. If someone needs Jesus, tell him about Jesus — *now*. I never went to a business gathering where Bill didn't, at some time during the meeting, put out the bait for somebody to come to church with him."

Then came the most moving comments of the day. Bill's business associate said he spent a lot of time with Bill during his bout with the cancer that would eventually claim his life. "I went to chemotherapy sessions with Bill," he said. "He hated the chemo, he hated the needles, but he loved the opportunity to talk to others with cancer about Christ."

He described going to visit Bill in the hospital one night just before Bill died. "I walked in and there was Bill in a drug-induced state. He didn't really know where he was. He didn't even know what day it was. There was his nurse with him; her name was Sophie. And Bill McMillen, lying there on his deathbed, was gently saying to her, 'So, Sophie ... when you die, do you know for sure that you're going to heaven?'"

The man paused as he fought back tears, then regained his composure. "Bill was working on Sophie," he said, "right up until the end."

Those were just a few of the stories that people told that day. They had to pass around boxes of tissues because of all the tears that flowed, though they were mixed with plenty of laughter too. I marveled at the number of people who will be in heaven for eternity because God found an ordinary but willing businessman named Bill McMillen to ambush them with his grace.

> We don't have to be preachers or theologians to make an eternal difference in the lives of others. Mainly, we just have to be willing.

Was Bill a bit quirky? You bet. But in a winsome way, with a wink and plenty of old-fashioned caring, Bill lived out a life that was overflowing with everyday evangelistic adventures.

And my bet is that today he doesn't regret a minute of it.

Action Principle ◄ · · · · · ·

We don't have to be preachers or theologians to make an eternal difference in the lives of others. Mainly, we just have to be willing. We can be ordinary people because we have an extraordinary message backed by an extraordinary God.

Stepping into the Adventure ◄ · · · · · ·

When Bill McMillen saw a spiritual need in someone's life, his instinctive response was to act, to do something about it right away. While he always saw himself as an ordinary individual who never felt totally adequate for the task, he learned that if he would take action, God would give him power as power was needed.

Consider Jesus in the garden of Gethsemane. He was overwhelmed with emotion over his impending death and all that would entail. He felt weak and fearful, but after ensuring that he was aligned with his Father's will, he obediently walked out of that garden, into the arms of his betrayer, and down the road toward Calvary. And God the Father made sure his Son had exactly what he needed to carry out his redemptive mission.

When you and I obey God, we're demonstrating faith. Faith isn't just believing something; it's believing something and taking action in accordance with that belief. Hebrews 11:6 says, "Without faith it is impossible to please God." But it's also true that *with* faith — that is, with the appropriate kinds of belief and obedience — we'll receive power as power is needed.

Bill McMillen knew the will of God when it came to evangelism. He had read all of the verses about being bearers of his light in a spiritually needy world. So when Bill encountered someone who needed Jesus, he put his faith into action. And as he followed God's will, he found himself empowered along the way to make an extraordinary impact.

How about you? Are you ordinary? Are you willing? Will you take one step today toward reaching someone for Christ? As you do, you'll find that God will come alongside of you and help you make the kind of eternal impact that nobody can make on his own.

> Inspiration for the Journey

I have fought the good fight, I have finished the race, I have kept the faith. Now there is in store for me the crown of righteousness, which the Lord, the righteous Judge, will award to me on that day — and not only to me, but also to all who have longed for his appearing.

2 Timothy 4:7 – 8

WORSHIP WITH CLASS

MARK MITTELBERG

"Let's try something different to make this more than just another typical class reunion," Fred said to me over the phone.

"I was thinking the same thing," I replied with a growing sense of excitement. "So many of our classmates have become Christians since graduation, including the two of us. Let's figure out a way we can all tell our stories and encourage our friends to consider trusting in Christ as well."

It was the first of several cross-country conversations with my friend from high school days, Fred Allen. In a dramatic turn of events, he had become a Jesus-follower several years out of school, about two years

> "Let's try something different to make this more than just another typical class reunion," Fred said to me.

after I had. Now we were approaching our ten-year class reunion and we thought it would be a good time to get the word out.

We realized that most class reunions are filled with talk of old times, catching up with former friends, a formal banquet, and a few unofficial parties — and usually alcohol everywhere to help everyone have "a good time." Yet the interactions are often superficial, with nobody getting down to the honest truth about how they're *really* doing, including what's working in their lives and what isn't.

As a result, reunions can be great fun, but they can also become lonely experiences that leave people feeling empty. We wanted to prevent that and turn this into an opportunity to encourage, go deep, and point our former schoolmates to Jesus, the best friend anyone can have.

As we looked at a draft of the reunion schedule, we saw a big hole in the weekend calendar: Sunday morning. Apparently, this was viewed as downtime after the banquet and late-night parties the evening before. It allowed everyone to sleep in (or "sleep it off") and come back rested for the final time together at the Sunday afternoon picnic.

"This is perfect," Fred said. "They've left Sunday morning totally open for us. Let's plan something that could become the best part of the whole reunion."

Since our town was in a fairly traditional region where church attendance was something you either did or felt guilty about not doing, we decided to take a straightforward approach and put together a Sunday morning church service. But we wanted to make it something our friends could relate to, regardless of their particular church (or nonchurch) background. So we scheduled it as late as possible on Sunday morning in order to keep it accessible to our more party-oriented pals.

We thought about what to call it, finally landing on "Worship with Class." That seemed to say it all. We were even able to secure the theater in our old school, which made our service the only event that would actually be on the school campus, giving people another reason to attend.

We needed to get the reunion committee's approval to make our service part of the official activities. Once the committee members knew that we were covering the expenses and doing all the work, they agreed to add it to the printed schedule and allowed us to insert a flyer into the packets given out at registration.

They even asked Fred, who had been our school president, to give an invocation at the Saturday night banquet, and they encouraged him while he was up front to invite everyone to attend Worship with Class. I think they were partially trying to support us, but they were also anxious to see the looks on everyone's faces when fun-loving-Fred, who never had a reputation for anything remotely religious, stood up to talk about God.

It certainly did get people's attention, and the next morning hundreds of our classmates, almost two-thirds of those attending the reunion, showed up for the service. Some came dressed in their "Sunday best," while other bleary-eyed buddies rolled in looking like they had skipped sleep altogether. The arrival of the latter group was, for me, the most rewarding part of the morning.

I hosted the service and Laud, a musician from our class who had recently become a worship pastor at a church, led the music. Chuck, one of our school's top athletes, and several others quickly assembled a vocal team and band. Sherry, who had been our homecoming queen, and Susie, one of our popular cheerleaders, gave brief testimonies — as did Fred and I and about half a dozen of our other classmates — of how Christ had changed our lives. Finally Fred gave a hard-hitting and engaging sermon on why we need the love, forgiveness, and leadership of Jesus in our lives.

Everyone seemed to be moved in one way or another by the experience. During the picnic afterwards, we kept hearing stories of how people had been encouraged and how meaningful it had been to hear what is really going on in their friends' lives. Some even confided that the service had given them a lot to think about as they considered the course of their own lives.

At the end of the day, everyone who put on the service was exhausted. But we felt "happy tired" because we knew we had seized a rare opportunity to tell friends we really cared about, and who in some cases we might never see again, about the love and grace of God.

In fact, the feedback was so positive that we determined to do something like it again at every reunion. Since then we've hosted Worship with Class II and Worship with Class III at subsequent gatherings, and at every event we encourage as many of our classmates as possible to stand up and tell their friends about the love and truth of Christ.

And it all started out of the desire to "try something different."

> Action Principle

When it comes to reaching people with the gospel, "Let's try something different" isn't a bad motto. Too often churches and individual Christians stick with worn-out approaches to speak to people who weren't reached by that same strategy the last time around. Our biblical message should never change, but our ways of communicating it must. Wise innovation and effective evangelism go hand in hand. Before we get too hung up on redeploying the old, we should consider what it means to genuinely follow the one who said, "Look, I am making all things new!" (Revelation 21:5 NLT).

> Our biblical message should never change, but our ways of communicating it must.

> Stepping into the Adventure

The apostle Paul said poignantly:

I have made myself a slave to everyone, to win as many as possible. To the Jews I became like a Jew, to win the Jews. To those under the law I became like one under the law (though I myself am not under the law), so as to win those under the law. To those not having the law I became like one not having the law (though I am not free from God's law but am under Christ's law), so as to win those not having the law. To the weak I became weak, to win the weak. I have become all things to all people so that by all possible means I might save some. I do all this for the sake of the gospel, that I may share in its blessings.

1 Corinthians 9:19 – 23 TNIV

Note that Paul was very clear about his goal to win everyone possible to faith in Christ. There was no ambiguity about what he was trying to accomplish, nor was there with Jesus, who said he came "to seek and to save what was lost" (Luke 19:10).

We need to embark on our journey with that same kind of clarity. Our goal in this great adventure should be to lovingly communicate the gospel to our family, friends, and others through our actions and our words, in ways God can use to draw them to Christ. It's never about manipulating someone to do something but rather winsomely encouraging folks to consider the forgiveness, friendship, and guidance God so graciously offers.

Once we're clear on the mission, God gives us a lot of latitude about how to accomplish it. The instructions are basically this: stay within God's biblical and moral parameters, seek his wisdom and guidance, act in love, and do everything you can to reach people for him.

So innovate. Experiment. Stretch yourself. Move outside your comfort zone. Try, fall down, get up, and try again. Find approaches that connect and use them as often as you can. Like Paul, we need to "become all things to all people so that by all possible means [we, with God's help] might save some."

⟩ Inspiration for the Journey

For you were once darkness, but now you are light in the Lord. Live as children of light (for the fruit of the light consists in all goodness, righteousness and truth) and find out what pleases the Lord.... Be very careful, then, how you live — not as unwise but as wise, making the most of every opportunity, because the days are evil.

Ephesians 5:8 – 10, 15 – 16

READY TO MAKE
A DIFFERENCE

LEE STROBEL

I had just returned from southern India, where I had snapped nearly two thousand color slides as our team traveled from Bombay (now Mumbai) to the southwestern province of Andhra Pradesh to participate in evangelistic rallies and medical relief efforts.

The staff at the newspaper where I was an editor didn't quite know what to think about my extracurricular adventure. Very few of them were committed Christians, so they didn't have a context to understand why their boss would spend his vacation in an impoverished area halfway around the globe. Like all good journalists, however, they displayed a healthy curiosity.

"Why don't you show us your slides?" a reporter asked me one day.

"Okay, good idea," I said. "I'll reserve the conference room over lunch one day next week. Anyone who's interested can bring something to eat, and I'll show the images on the wall."

The reporter hesitated. "Umm, I don't mean *all* your slides," he said, just to make sure.

"Right," I replied. "I'll edit it down to the best ones."

More than a dozen staff members showed up that day, brown bag lunches in hand, and we sat around an elongated table to eat. They seemed genuinely interested in finding out what happened during my month-long trip, especially since I had returned twenty-two pounds lighter.

One by one, I began clicking through the slides. Beautiful scenes of vast and lush wilderness. Depressing images of naked children playing in open sewage ditches in the slums of Bombay. A seemingly endless number of homeless people rolled up in thin blankets as they slept on the sidewalks of Hyderabad. Colorful pictures of bustling marketplaces. Vivid portraits of women clad in bright red, yellow, and blue saris, lugging jugs of water through a rural village. Disturbing photos of polio victims on the dirt floor of their grass huts.

I gave a running commentary as the slides flashed on the wall, although I steered clear of many spiritual references. I didn't want to be accused of abusing my position as a supervisor by proselytizing my staff on company premises. I did, however, feel the freedom to answer any questions that came up.

Toward the end of my presentation, I showed several slides of the thousands of people who crowded into outdoor venues at our evening rallies. Then I closed with pictures of joyful new believers waist deep in the slate gray Krishna River.

"These people have just become Christians," I said, showing a succession of images of them being immersed in the water and then emerging triumphantly. "Here they're being baptized — ironically, in a river named after a Hindu deity."

I let the last slide linger for a few moments and then flipped on the lights to a spattering of applause. "Well, that's it," I said. "Any questions before we get back to work?"

I wasn't sure what to expect. Then one of the reporters, an

earnest and hardworking journeyman, half raised his hand. He had a puzzled look on his face.

"You indicated those people in the water had 'become Christians,'" he began, emphasizing those last two words. "What does it mean to *become* a Christian? I thought you were sort of born that way. Like in America — you're born here, so you're automatically a Christian, right?"

Whoa! What an incredible opportunity! All eyes in the room shot to me. Everyone, it seemed, was eager to hear the answer.

> I had one hundred and twenty seconds to explain to a group of inquisitive but generally irreligious journalists what it means to become a Christian.

I glanced at the clock: it was two minutes before one o'clock, which meant I had one hundred and twenty seconds to explain to a group of inquisitive but generally irreligious journalists what it means to become a Christian.

Freeze that moment. Put yourself in my shoes. What would you have said?

As you think about that, let me fast-forward a few years to another scene. By then I had left my newspaper career and was a new staff member at a large church outside of Chicago, where one of my roles was to handle inquiries from the news media. One day a reporter from my former newspaper came to the church to do an article on our fast-growing congregation. I set up an interview for him with our associate pastor, who asked me to sit in the room during their conversation so I could be aware of the kind of topics the reporter was pursuing.

The interview was going well. For twenty minutes or so, the journalist asked good though rather predictable questions. I was sitting in a chair near the door, and after a while was only half listening and fighting off drowsiness.

Then, without warning, the reporter startled me by suddenly turning in his chair to face me squarely. "So, Lee," he said, "what's *your* story?"

Freeze that moment too. Imagine that an inquiring interviewer, out of the blue, asks you to recount your testimony about becoming a follower of Christ. His pen is poised, ready to take down your words and print them for thousands of people to read. Quick, what would *you* say?

I'm grateful that before those two reporters asked me those questions, someone had given me basic training on how to share my faith with others. Without that background and the confidence that comes with it, I would have found myself fumbling for replies and inevitably frustrating the person I had a chance to reach.

Usually, these kinds of opportunities arise without warning. There's no way to call a "time out." Just as wise adventurers prepare thoroughly before they head off to climb a mountain or explore a sunken ship, we need to do enough advance work so that we will instinctively be ready to engage with our friends when the door opens to a spiritual conversation.

> Action Principle

Unexpected adventures are, well, *unexpected.* So the time to get prepared is *now*, not when you're already sitting down with someone who surprises you with his or her sudden receptivity to the gospel. In fact, here's a little-known Law of Evangelism: the better we're equipped, the more God seems to use us. It's almost as if he is reluctant to inflict us on others when we're not appropriately trained.

> The better we're equipped, the more God seems to use us.

Stepping into the Adventure ←·····

I remember when Mark and I were asked to train a class of seminary students on how to tell others about Jesus in simple, everyday ways. We were stunned that even though they were on the verge of graduating and becoming pastors, many of them were unable to clearly articulate their testimony in three minutes and in plain English.

One student got terribly flustered as we worked with him to purge his story of "Christianese." Finally, he declared in frustration, "If I take out the Christian clichés, I won't have anything left to say."

The key is *training*, not just information or inspiration. Reading a book like this one can heighten your motivation for evangelism, but the next step is to systematically prepare yourself for the unexpected opportunities to share Christ with others.

Mark and I partnered with Bill Hybels in developing the updated DVD-based *Becoming a Contagious Christian Training Course* in order to equip you to tell your testimony clearly and succinctly — not as a canned presentation but as a natural and easy-to-follow story that others can relate to. You'll also learn how to do everything from starting spiritual conversations to leading someone across the line of faith to explaining the gospel in straightforward ways that everybody can understand. One of the illustrations the course teaches is what I used in answering the reporter's question about how a person becomes a Christian.

"Christianity is different from all other faiths," I began. "Other religions are spelled D-O, meaning people have to *do* good deeds, like praying in certain ways, being extra nice to others, or giving money to the poor to try to earn their way to God. The problem is, they never know how many good deeds they need to do. And

>rse, the Bible says they can never do enough to merit eternal life.

"But Christianity is spelled D-O-N-E. Jesus has *done* for us what we could never do for ourselves. He lived the perfect life and died as our substitute to pay for all of our wrongdoing. He offers forgiveness and eternal life as a free gift that nobody can earn. But merely knowing this isn't enough. We must receive Jesus as our forgiver and leader. *That's* how a person becomes a Christian."

I'm glad I was taught that illustration and others in a safe setting where I could practice among friends and get my mistakes out of the way. That's the beauty of going through the *Contagious* training or some other course in a small group or seminar.

Mark likes to compare this training to the preparation a pilot goes through before he takes command of a commercial jet. "When you're trusting your life to someone flying a plane," he says, "aren't you glad he did all his crashing in the flight simulator first?"

Similarly, your inquiring friend is going to be grateful that you "crashed and burned" a few times as you practiced your testimony and various gospel illustrations in the safety of a training course. That way, you'll be prepared and confident to help him at that crucial moment when he becomes open to hearing about Christ.

> Inspiration for the Journey

Therefore, prepare your minds for action; be self-controlled; set your hope fully on the grace to be given you when Jesus Christ is revealed.

1 Peter 1:13

SPIRITUAL BACKUP

MARK MITTELBERG

We had been in Orlando leading an event called the Contagious Evangelism Conference. After a couple of days of teaching, encouraging leaders, responding to questions, and dealing with countless details, our team was in dire need of rest. The problem was that we had to rush to the airport to catch a late flight back to Chicago, so there was no slowing down until we were finally on the airplane.

As we boarded, I was relieved to discover that Lee and I had been assigned adjacent seats. We were frankly too relationally fatigued to feel like interacting with strangers. It was good to know we'd be able to relax, chat about the conference, and get a little rest.

Our friend Andy, who had helped lead the conference, wasn't so "lucky." He was in the row immediately in front of us, seated next to a stranger who turned out to be extremely extroverted and anxious to talk (and talk …). Normally that's a good thing, but we knew Andy must have been as tired as we were.

Lee and I didn't pay much attention to them or their conversation, which was mostly drowned out by the airplane noise and chatter. We just talked with each other about how things had gone in Florida, enjoyed our "meal" of pretzels and a soft drink, and gradually got ready for the naps that would inevitably follow.

I leaned back in my seat and settled in for some serious shut-eye. By this time the airplane noise had subsided somewhat, and I couldn't help but hear a bit of the interaction Andy was having with his newfound friend.

As I tuned in for a moment, I realized they were engaged in a fairly deep spiritual conversation. In fact, the man — who turned out to be an atheist — was raising a variety of questions and objections related to the Christian faith, and Andy was patiently responding to each of his challenges.

Way to go, Andy. I thought to myself as a wave of exhaustion began to overtake me. *Lord, please use Andy as he tries to point this guy toward your love and truth,* I prayed as I slipped off to sleep. I'm not sure I even completed the thought or said a proper "amen." I found out later that Lee had been in the process of doing the same thing.

Meanwhile, Andy was faithfully doing his best to field a greater number of spiritual challenges than he'd encountered in a long time — and perhaps never in such rapid-fire fashion. He found himself drawing from the far reaches of his memory to recall things he had read in the Bible and various apologetics books, learned in philosophy classes at his Christian college, and heard in sermons at church.

He kept reassuring himself that he wasn't alone.

Throughout this conversation, Andy later informed us, he kept reassuring himself that he wasn't alone. *I've got Lee Strobel and Mark Mittelberg in the seats immediately behind me,* he told himself. *If this guy comes up with an objection I've never heard or a ques-*

*tion I can't answer, then these guys — who are probably listening
with rapt attention at this very moment — will lean forward and
provide whatever information or answers are necessary. Lee and
Mark are known for writing and speaking about these things all
over the world, and now I've got the two of them backing me up.*

I'm not sure whether Andy turned around in the hope of
getting an approving nod or an affirming thumbs-up or whether
he finally heard one of us snoring, but when Andy finally did
nonchalantly glance over his shoulder, he was disappointed to
discover that his spiritual comrades-in-arms were comatose.

At first Andy felt let down. *A lot of help these guys are,* he
thought. *They teach crowds of people about evangelism, and then
they can't even stay awake long enough to give a buddy a little
spiritual support.*

But then something occurred to him: he had just answered
the guy's questions and presented the message of Christianity on
his own. He may not have done it exactly the way Lee or Mark
would have done it, but who cares? Maybe he had done it better.

More importantly, maybe the evangelistic "backup" he had
been banking on had already been provided by God, but in a
much more direct and powerful way than we ever could have offered. Perhaps what Andy had needed was not the assistance of
a couple of guys who teach about reaching others but rather the
guidance and affirmation of the One who invented the concept
and commissioned it in the first place. *He* knows the heart and
mind of this atheist next to Andy and loves him more than any
of us ever could.

Jesus told his followers:

> But the Counselor, the Holy Spirit, whom the Father will
> send in my name, will teach you all things and will remind
> you of everything I have said to you. Peace I leave with you;

my peace I give you. I do not give to you as the world gives. Do not let your hearts be troubled and do not be afraid....

But I tell you the truth: It is for your good that I am going away. Unless I go away, the Counselor will not come to you; but if I go, I will send him to you. When he comes, he will convict the world of guilt in regard to sin and righteousness and judgment (John 14:26 – 27; 16:7 – 8).

I don't know if that man took further steps to figure things out or to consider the truths he heard during the flight that night. But I'm glad Andy was there when Lee and I weren't, and that every one of us has the promise of the Holy Spirit's power, guidance, and wisdom to help us make the most of every unexpected spiritual adventure.

> Action Principle

When we prayerfully venture out and tell God's story to the people around us, we're never alone. We've got "spiritual backup" from the all-knowing, all-powerful, ever-present, ultra-loving Creator of the universe. So speak boldly in the confidence that he is not only *with* you, he's more than willing to *help* you communicate his life-giving message to the people around you.

> Stepping into the Adventure

There's an old-but-true saying that warrants repeating: whatever God expects, God enables. In other words, he doesn't ask us to do anything that he won't also give us the ability and resources to accomplish.

If this is true, what does it tell us about Jesus' famous instructions that he gave his disciples — and therefore to us — right before his ascension into heaven? He said in Matthew 28:19 – 20:

"Therefore go and make disciples of all nations, baptizing them in the name of the Father and of the Son and of the Holy Spirit, and teaching them to obey everything I have commanded you." These words make up what is commonly referred to as the Great Commission. But were they merely a lofty expression of wishful-but-unrealistic thinking, or did Jesus back up his Great Commission with his Great Provision in order to make it attainable?

Whatever God expects, God enables.

We can find answers by applying the basic rule of sound Bible study: examine the *context*, which refers to the verses immediately around the passage we're studying. When we do this, we find encouragement in Jesus' words right before and after his famous command.

The first example is in verse 18, where he begins by saying, "All authority in heaven and on earth has been given to me," which builds our confidence greatly about who is telling us to "therefore go and make disciples." And in the verse right after this command, Jesus assures us by adding this promise: "And surely I am with you always, to the very end of the age."

What does that mean for you and me today? Simply that as we obey his Great Commission, we never do so in our own strength or authority. The same one who is the Commander is also the Provider, and he'll literally be with us, enabling us to obey his words and giving us assurance that we'll have impact as we embark on the adventure of telling others about his amazing love and truth.

> Inspiration for the Journey

His divine power has given us everything we need for life and godliness through our knowledge of him who called us by his own glory and goodness.

2 Peter 1:3

PASSION FOR PEOPLE

LEE STROBEL

He was Jewish, a comedian by profession, but the situation at the time was far from funny. In fact, as our impromptu debate kept heating up, with our voices getting louder and louder and the crowd around us getting bigger and bigger, an off-duty FBI agent felt compelled to step in because he was afraid that we were going to come to blows.

Oh, well, just another night at a Christian outreach event.

Actually, that evening had been unusual from the beginning. With Easter approaching, Mark and I had invited one of the world's leading experts on the resurrection of Jesus to speak at our church on a Sunday night.

We encouraged Christians to bring their spiritually interested friends to hear Dr. Gary Habermas, who wrote *The Historical Jesus* and later co-authored *The Case for the Resurrection of Jesus*, but we were skeptical about how many would be willing to attend a weekend lecture by a college professor. The auditorium had seats for 4,500, and we roped off everything except for five hundred chairs right in front of the stage. Then we prayed fervently that we would be able to fill those.

Shortly before the event, our prayers were answered. A reporter for the *Chicago Tribune* quoted a notorious local atheist as saying he was going to show up and pepper Habermas with tough objections during the question-and-answer time. That set off an incredible buzz in the community, which I had fun highlighting during the Sunday morning services. "It's going to be a hot time in the ol' auditorium tonight," I assured them.

That evening, we watched in amazement as throngs of people poured into that auditorium, filling it beyond capacity with just over five thousand people. Habermas surveyed the vast audience before he went up on the platform. "I've never spoken to this many people!" he declared.

Ironically, the intrepid atheist ended up oversleeping his nap and missed the entire event. I did, however, later send him a note to thank him for attracting so many people to hear the evidence for Jesus rising from the dead. "You've influenced more people for Christ than a lot of Christians I know," I joked. (He was an old friend from my atheist days, so I knew he could handle the kidding.)

Everything at the event went smoothly. Habermas gave an excellent presentation of the historical data for the resurrection and then adroitly fielded questions for half an hour. At the end, Mark challenged visitors to continue to investigate the powerful evidence they had heard and come to their own verdict on whether the case for the resurrection was believable.

Afterward, people were milling around the auditorium. I was standing in one of the aisles, looking for a friend of mine, when the Jewish comedian accosted me. He had arrived late, missing most of the event, but he was adamant about getting answers to his objections concerning the resurrection.

"Hey, you were part of this event," he said to me in an accusatory and belligerent tone. "How can you propagate this mythology about a resurrection? How can you claim there's any evidence to back up what is obviously a fable? This is ridiculous!"

"Whoa!" I replied, trying to calm him down. "Do you have a specific question I can help you with?"

"Specific question?" he nearly shouted back at me. "Yeah, like a hundred of them. Are you saying I'm going to hell because I don't believe in a two-thousand-year-old fairy tale?"

His aggressive and argumentative demeanor quickly attracted the attention of people around us. Pretty soon, a crowd began to form, surrounding us as if we were two kids about to duke it out on the elementary school playground.

I did my best to answer his question, but as soon as I got a rudimentary response out of my mouth, he quickly moved on to other objections: people can't come back from the dead; it's medically impossible. Maybe Jesus didn't even die on the cross. Or the disciples stole his body. You can't trust the Gospels; they were written too long after Jesus lived. And on and on.

More than I had intended, I began to match his pugnacious tone as I tried to respond to his questions. My voice got louder to match his. The crowd grew and grew. That's when one of the ushers, an FBI agent who volunteered to help with security, moved in, ready to intervene because he thought a fight was going to break out.

The comedian and I went back and forth for half an hour. Then he did the unexpected: he abruptly smiled and stuck out his hand in a gesture of friendship. "Thanks for being willing to argue with me," he said. "I really appreciate that you stood up for what you believe."

"What do you mean?" I asked.

"I've been to a bunch of priests and pastors and ministers, and

"Thanks for being willing to argue with me," he said. "I really appreciate that you stood up for what you believe."

when I'd raise an argument against the resurrection, they'd just smile and say, 'Well, touché. That's a good point,' and they'd walk away. They wouldn't defend what they believe, and it made me mad. If they were going to teach it, why wouldn't they defend it? I started to wonder whether anybody believed in this Christianity stuff enough to debate it."

"Look," I said as I shook his hand, "I'm sorry I got a little too adamant."

"No," he exclaimed. "That's what I needed. I *needed* to argue about this. I really appreciate the fact that you're passionate about what you believe." And now, he said, he was going to be more willing to calmly search for answers.

I look back on that incident with mixed emotions. In retrospect, I didn't handle the confrontation with the full measure of gentleness that 1 Peter 3:15 says we should display in answering questions. However, what I lacked in my demeanor I think I made up for in passion, and it turned out that was exactly what this man had been looking for. And frankly, he's right: if Christianity *is* true — and if Jesus *did* confirm his divinity by rising from the dead — then Christians ought to be enthusiastic about the resurrection and fervent in our defense of this cornerstone of our faith.

Otherwise, we send signals to people like this comedian that we don't care much, one way or the other. And if we don't, why should *they*?

> Action Principle

Christians who lack conviction have little to communicate to others. People see no reason to get excited about Jesus if Christians aren't. But when we're enthusiastic about our faith, this tells seekers and skeptics that we are truly captivated by Christ. As

German philosopher Georg Hegel said, "Nothing great in the world has ever been accomplished without passion."[17]

Stepping into the Adventure

Mark and I were sitting in the front row during a Sunday service at a great cathedral in Europe. The architecture and stained glass were magnificent; the rich organ music echoed through the cavernous sanctuary. The pastor, decked out in an opulent robe, was preaching from an elevated pulpit. But clearly something was lacking.

I leaned over to Mark. "He doesn't believe one word he's saying," I whispered.

Maybe that was a bit unfair. But everything about the way he talked about Jesus — with a bland monotone voice devoid of energy, emotion, or conviction — told me he was merely going through the motions. I doubted if any spiritual seekers would get excited about his message since he so obviously was not.

When I was a child, my parents would take me to their church. The organist played the right notes, but there was no passion behind the music. The sermons droned. People dutifully repeated the Apostles' Creed as if they were reciting baseball statistics of teams they didn't care about.

None of this made sense to me. If the Christian story is true — in all its splendor, glory, and wonder — then shouldn't Christians be fired up about it? Shouldn't they be anxious to tell others about Christ? Shouldn't they at least *smile*? Instead, the look on their faces convinced me they were merely fulfilling some sort of antiquated or obligatory religious requirement. If their faith seems so dead, I told myself, then maybe it's because Jesus really is dead.

I'm not saying we should manufacture phony or hyped emotions. But if we don't walk away from our daily experience with

Jesus excited about his presence in our lives, then something's awry. If we aren't excited by the single most important message ever delivered to humankind, then what *will* energize us?

We can be passionate without being obnoxious; we can be enthused about Christ without making fools of ourselves. But our faith won't be very contagious until we ourselves are thoroughly imbued with the passion of following Jesus.

> Our faith won't be very contagious until we ourselves are thoroughly imbued with the passion of following Jesus.

"Seekers have little respect for weak Christians," said Bill Hybels and Mark Mittelberg in *Becoming a Contagious Christian.* "Deep down they're looking for somebody — anybody — to step up and proclaim the truth and then to live it boldly. And I just have to ask: why can't that be you and me?"[18]

> Inspiration for the Journey

[Christ] sent me to tell the Good News, and to tell it without using the language of human wisdom, in order to make sure that Christ's death on the cross is not robbed of its power.

1 Corinthians 1:17 GNT

THE UNSEEN SIDE OF THE JOURNEY

MARK MITTELBERG

"I had a strange dream last night," Barb, my coworker, confided to me as we were getting ready to close up shop. She was trying to act casual about it, but I could tell this was something serious. "You and your friend who comes into the store once in a while — that really nice guy with the dark hair — were both in it."

"Really?" I replied, showing more interest than she was probably expecting. "What were we doing in your dream?"

"That's what is so interesting," she said. "All I know is that you were both talking to me. I don't remember what you were saying, but it seemed *really* important."

I had been a follower of Christ for only a few days at that point, so I was half expecting miracles everywhere I looked. Working in an electronics store and just beginning to figure out what it means to be a Christian in the marketplace, I wanted to perform well in my job, but more than anything I wanted to make a difference for God.

"I had a strange dream last night," Barb, my coworker, confided to me as we were getting ready to close up shop.

"Are you talking about Dave Roise, who was in here several days ago, talking to me over by the counter?" I asked, wanting to make sure we were talking about the same friend.

"That's the guy," she said. "Isn't it weird that I'd have a dream about you two, especially when I've barely met Dave and didn't even know his name?"

"It might be unusual, but I don't think it's weird. It might actually mean something," I said.

"Like what?" she asked.

"Listen, you need to close out the cash register and I need to turn off the lights and equipment. This conversation is important; let's pick it up again after work, when we can really talk about it."

Barb's casual expression was now gone, replaced by a mix of curiosity and concern. "Okay," she replied, a bit hesitantly.

We took care of our duties and went out for a soft drink. "Listen, Barb," I said, trying to be sensitive, "I'm not trying to overreact to a dream, but here's what made it so interesting to me. That friend you mentioned, Dave, is a really strong Christian. Did you know that?"

"No," she replied, looking at me quizzically. "So what does that mean?"

"Well, there's something else I don't think you know: I committed my own life to Christ a few days ago, and I'm really serious about following and serving God now."

This came as a real shock to Barb, partly because she had observed some of my wilder party-oriented side, but also because it was dawning on her what the common link was between Dave and me.

"And not only that," I added, "but Dave was one of the people who had an influence on my decision to become a Christian."

"So I had a dream about two guys," she said, "and I didn't realize that either of you are, like, serious Christians."

"And what we said to you in the dream was *really* important," I piped in.

"What did you say to me?" she asked innocently.

"Well, I don't know. I wasn't actually there — in your dream," I reminded her with a smile, trying to lighten things up a little. "But could it be that God was speaking to you, giving you a sign by telling you to listen to our message?"

"Wow" was about all Barb got out for the next moment or two.

"And our message," I added, "would be about God's love for you. And his desire for you to come to him and receive the forgiveness that Jesus paid for by dying on the cross. He did this for all of us — for Dave, me, *and* you — in fact, for everyone who will ask for it and humbly turn from their own ways to follow him."

"Wow," she managed to say again. "That's a lot to think about."

"It is," I said. "I had wanted to talk to you about this, though I wasn't going to hit you with so much, so fast. But maybe God wanted to go ahead and stir things up sooner, so he gave you this cool dream."

Barb nodded.

"I would encourage you to do what you just said: really think about it. And pray about it too, asking God to show you that it's true. If you'd like, you can come to the Bible study that I've started going to on Monday nights with Dave and a bunch of other great people, and we can talk about your questions, and — "

"Whoa, boy! Slow down!" Barb interjected, humored by my untethered zeal. "I'm still trying to get over the dream part."

"I'm sorry. I just get all fired up about what I've found and how I feel, knowing I'm forgiven and that God is using me to talk to people about him," I said. "I'll try to slow down. And I'll pray for you as you try to figure it all out. I'm new at this, but I'd be happy to talk about it more whenever you want to."

"I'm sensing that," Barb said lightheartedly, but still with a hint of caution. "Thanks." We finished our drinks and conversation, saying good-bye until the next day of work.

Barb committed her life to Christ a few weeks later, and she became a close friend as we figured out, side by side, how to live for Christ and how to share him with the people around us. Oddly enough, it all started with a dream that I'm convinced came from the author of evangelism himself. The unexpected adventure was *his* idea. We get to join him in what he's already up to, hanging on for the ride of our lives as he works behind the scenes, touching people around us in astounding ways.

> Action Principle

The Holy Spirit is our invisible guide in this amazing journey of sharing our faith with others. He piques people's interest, warms their hearts, informs their minds, opens their eyes, and sometimes even infuses their imaginations with redemptive dreams and ideas — and then he opens up opportunities and guides us on how we can make the most of them. That's why we can pray, prepare, and step out boldly. We're simply joining God in his outreach enterprise, reaching a world of people about whom he is "patient ... not wanting anyone to perish, but everyone to come to repentance" (2 Peter 3:9).

> Stepping into the Adventure

I love the idea of God's behind-the-scenes spiritual activities, but I honestly find it hard to expect them day to day. I don't know if it's our secular culture that makes me skeptical or my own evangelical background which tends to relegate the supernatural to the pages of the Bible. Either way, it's easy for me—and perhaps for you—to slip into thinking that spiritual transformation comes down to us, what *we* say and do to bring people to faith in Christ.

That's why we need to hear stories like this one about Barb to remind us that there's much more to the adventure than meets the eye. We're part of a cosmic drama unfolding on this planet, and we get to be in the center of the action, on the front lines of *God's* activity. He "routinely" works in ways that would astound us if we were to really comprehend them. Yes, he uses our words and actions, but his activities go far beyond what we can say or do.

Just look at Acts 10, where God launched a completely unexpected adventure by sending an angel to prepare Cornelius and then used a dream to instruct Peter to go to him and explain the gospel. The result was that all the members of Cornelius's household put their faith in Christ, were filled with the Holy Spirit, and were baptized—all in a single day.

God still uses dreams to reach people. "I've spoken in many Islamic countries, where it's tough to talk about Jesus," Indian-born apologist Ravi Zacharias told Lee Strobel for his book *The Case for Faith*. "Virtually every Muslim who has come to follow Christ has done so, first, because of the love of Christ expressed through a Christian, or second, because of a vision, a dream, or some other supernatural intervention."[19] Indeed, one of the greatest Indian converts from Sikhism, Sadhu Sundar Singh, who once tore the pages out of the Bible one by one and burned them, became a Christian missionary after Christ appeared to him in a dream.

> Remember that we serve a supernatural God who is not limited in the ways he can work.

Remember that we serve a supernatural God who is not limited in the ways he can work. If he has done it before, he can do it again — except this time using *you* in the middle of the action.

> Inspiration for the Journey

Unless I go away, the Counselor will not come to you; but if I go, I will send him to you. When he comes, he will convict the world of guilt in regard to sin and righteousness and judgment.

John 16:7 – 8

OUTRAGEOUS GRACE

LEE STROBEL

"This is embarrassing," my friend said to me over the phone.

"That's okay," I assured him. "Go ahead. You can tell me."

He sighed. "Well, we found out our little girl shoplifted a book from the church bookstore. We were really surprised because she's a good kid. Anyway, I was wondering whether you would help us out with something."

Frankly, I was relieved the news wasn't more serious. "Sure," I said. "What can I do?"

"We'd like you to represent the church so she can come in and apologize," he replied. "Maybe you could figure out some sort of restitution. We want to use this as a teaching moment."

I agreed to help, but I have to admit I had an even bigger lesson in mind.

The next day, the parents and their eight-year-old daughter walked hesitantly into my office and sat down. The girl was so small, she was almost swallowed up by the chair. Her eyes were downcast; her mood was somber.

After I exchanged some pleasantries with her parents, I sat

down on the edge of my desk so I was facing the girl. As gently as I could, I said to her, "Tell me what happened."

She hesitated, her lower lip quivering. "Well," she said as she started to sniffle, "I was in the bookstore after a service and I saw a book that I really wanted, but I didn't have any money."

Now tears pooled in her eyes and spilled down her cheeks. I handed her a tissue, which she used to dab her eyes before continuing.

"So I put the book under my coat and took it," she blurted out, almost as if she wanted to expel the words as fast as she could so they wouldn't linger. "I knew it was wrong. I knew I shouldn't do it, but I did it. And I'm sorry. I'll never do it again. Honest."

She was so contrite that it broke my heart. "I'm glad you're willing to admit what you did and say you're sorry," I told her. "That's very brave, and it's the right thing to do."

She nodded slightly.

"But," I continued, "what do you think an appropriate punishment would be?"

She shrugged her shoulders. I knew from her parents that she had already thrown out the book to hide the evidence. I paused for a moment, then said, "I understand the book cost five dollars. I think it would be fair if you paid the bookstore five dollars, plus three times that amount, which would make the total twenty dollars. Do you think that would be fair?"

"Yes," she murmured, though I could see fear — almost panic — in her eyes. Her mind was whirring. *Where was she going to come up with twenty dollars?* That's a mountain of money for a little kid. She didn't have the five dollars to buy the book in the first place, and suddenly her debt had spiraled completely out of sight.

At that moment, I got up and walked behind my desk. Sitting

down, I pulled open the top drawer. The little girl's eyes narrowed. She couldn't figure out what I was doing.

I pulled out my checkbook, picked up a pen, and wrote a check from my personal account for the full amount that she owed. I tore off the check and held it in my hand. Her mouth dropped open.

"I know there's no way you can pay the penalty that you deserve," I told her. "So I'm going to pay it for you. Do you know why I'd do that?"

Bewildered, she shook her head.

"Because I love you," I told her. "Because I care about you. Because you're important to me. And please remember this: that's how Jesus feels about you too. Except even *more*."

With that, I handed her the check, which she grabbed and clutched to her heart. She simply blossomed with a look of absolute relief and joy and wonder. She was almost giddy with gratitude. The same little girl who had slinked into the office under the weight of shame now left lighthearted and skipping.

I don't know how God ultimately used that teaching moment in her life. But I do know this: once a person, even at a young age, experiences a taste of the kind of grace offered by Christ, it leaves an indelible mark on the soul. Who could resist being attracted by the forgiveness and unmerited favor extended by Jesus?

This is one of the greatest dimensions of the unexpected adventure. The message we convey isn't based on condemnation or shame. We're not offering people a life sentence of hard labor to try to somehow make themselves worthy of heaven. Instead, we have the privilege of telling people how they can find complete forgiveness as a free gift that was purchased

> Once a person, even at a young age, experiences a taste of the kind of grace offered by Christ, it leaves an indelible mark on the soul.

when Jesus died as our substitute to pay for all of our wrongdoing — past, present, and future.

"Grace means there's nothing we can do to make God love us more," writes Philip Yancey in his classic book *What's So Amazing About Grace?* "And grace means there's nothing we can do to make God love us less.... Grace means that God already loves us as much as an infinite God can possibly love."[20]

Wow! When I try to let that sink in, I'm just as overcome with gratitude as that little girl. At the same time I feel a renewed desire to let others know about this incredible message of redemption and reconciliation. After all, with good news like that, how could we possibly keep it to ourselves?

> Action Principle

Some people come bearing bad news: the surgeon after an unsuccessful operation, the IRS agent announcing an audit, the bank officer turning down a loan. But fortunately, we don't have to bring disappointment and grief to others; instead, we have a hopeful and optimistic message of forgiveness, grace, a meaningful life, and heaven. That ought to be enough to make the task of evangelism a mission of joy.

> Stepping into the Adventure

Often when we've been Christians for a long time, we begin to lose our childlike wonder of God's grace. *Amazing* grace becomes *interesting* grace and then, well ... it's merely a word in a verse. But sometimes we catch a fresh glimpse of the magnitude of God's forgiveness and once again we vicariously experience what it's like to have a lifetime of guilt lifted off our shoulders.

This happened to me at one of our baptism services at a church where I was a pastor. During the ceremony, we asked participants to write down their sins on a piece of paper. When they came onto the platform, they would pin the paper to a giant cross. This is reflective of Colossians 2:14, which says of God: "He canceled the record that contained the charges against us. He took it and destroyed it by nailing it to Christ's cross" (NLT).

After the service, one young woman wrote a letter in which she recounted her experience:

> I remember my fear — *the most fear I ever remember* — as I wrote as tiny as I could on a piece of paper the word *abortion*. I was scared someone would open up the paper and read it and find out it was me. I almost wanted to walk out of the auditorium during the service, the guilt and fear were that strong.
>
> When my turn came, I walked up toward the center of the stage toward the cross and pinned the paper there and was directed over toward a pastor to be baptized. He looked me straight in the eyes. And I thought for sure he was going to read in my eyes the terrible secret I had kept from everybody for so long.
>
> But instead, I felt like God was telling me, *I love you. It's okay. You are forgiven. You are forgiven!* I felt so much love for me — a terrible sinner. That's the first time I had ever really *felt* forgiveness and unconditional love. It was unbelievable, and it was indescribable.

She's right — it *is* unbelievable! Think back to the moment when you first felt God's complete and total forgiveness wash over you, cleansing you of your shame and guilt. Do you recall the emotion? Can you remember how light and liberated you felt when you were cut free from the anchor of sin? How did you react when God's promise from Isaiah 1:18 registered in your soul for the first time: "Though your sins are like scarlet, they shall be as white as snow; though they are red as crimson, they shall be like wool"?

Keep that incredible feeling alive inside of you, and let it spur you on in your unexpected adventure of spreading God's grace to others.

› Inspiration for the Journey

For it is by grace you have been saved, through faith — and this not from yourselves, it is the gift of God — not by works, so that no one can boast. For we are God's workmanship, created in Christ Jesus to do good works, which God prepared in advance for us to do.

Ephesians 2:8 – 10

POWER OF THE GOSPEL

MARK MITTELBERG

I had been teaching a group of church leaders from all over the country and around the world for a couple of hours before we took a mid-morning break. My topic was how pastors and leaders could help church members clarify their own spiritual stories, including how they made their commitments to Christ and the difference that has produced in their lives.

We had enjoyed great interactions, including a lively time of questions and answers, and then during the break I chatted with people who wanted to discuss things further. As we were nearing the time when we needed to start the workshop again, a man who had been waiting stepped up to say something to me.

"I'm a bit troubled by something you've been talking about," Steve began, "and I wondered if you could help me sort it out."

"I'd be happy to try," I said. "What's your concern?"

"Well," he replied, "you've been describing the Christian life with phrases like 'becoming a believer' and 'the point when a person trusts in Christ.' But some of us come from faith traditions that don't really talk that way. We don't emphasize conversion experiences or spiritual crisis points in a person's life. We tend to talk more about simply growing up in the faith, believing in God, participating in the church, and so forth. So given our emphasis, how would you apply what you've been teaching this morning to our situation?"

"That's a great question," I began, "because I know there really is a difference in how various groups of Christians describe what needs to happen in a person's life. Some parts of the church world emphasize the importance of a person having a dramatic moment of turning from sin to follow Christ. Others stress the need for people to understand this increasingly over time, leading them to embrace Christ during the process of learning about the truths of Christianity. And if that can happen naturally as a child grows up, it can lead to a consistent and stable faith."

Steve nodded affirmingly.

"But I do need to caution," I added, "that it's not always just a matter of semantics or emphasis. Sometimes I think people feel uncomfortable with talking about conversion or 'making a commitment to Christ' because in reality they've never actually taken that step themselves. In fact, I think there are a lot of people in churches who have just jumped on a bandwagon, which is easy to do these days when so many churches have such great bands. But they've never really internalized the message and asked Jesus to become their own forgiver and leader — "

Steve suddenly *burst into tears*. He was fairly discreet about it, but he didn't try to hide that I had hit a nerve. As he regained his composure, he attempted to explain why he thought my words had touched him at such a deep level. I encouraged him and listened as he spoke.

I soon realized, however, that we were a couple of minutes past the allotted time for the break and that most of the group were already back in the room, getting ready for me to start teaching again.

So I said, "Steve, this is obviously a very important discussion, and I don't want to shortchange it by trying to finish it quickly right this moment. Immediately after this next session, we're going to take a longer lunch break. Can we get together then and keep talking?"

Steve agreed. As soon as our group broke for lunch, he and I dashed to my car to drive to a nearby sandwich shop. Knowing the time would go quickly, we jumped back into our discussion as we drove.

Steve described to me what he had been realizing all morning, which was what I'd suspected. He had been involved for years in a variety of church programs and activities, but he had never actually asked Jesus to be his Savior. Steve was religious, but he didn't have a real relationship with Christ. This had now become clear in his mind, and for obvious reasons it was very troubling to him.

As I parked the car next to a deli, I tried to impress upon him that many people are in this situation and that he didn't need to feel embarrassed. But I also urged him not to stay in that situation any longer. I told him I believed God had led him to our workshop to hear the truth, and that God was graciously opening Steve's eyes to his need to receive the salvation Jesus paid for by dying on the cross.

> Steve was religious, but he didn't have a real relationship with Christ.

As I explained the gospel, Steve readily agreed with all that I said, and tears welled up in his eyes again as he affirmed that he wanted to know that he was forgiven for his sins and had become a true member of God's family.

"Steve," I said, "you can seal that decision right now by praying with me, right here, to receive God's gift of grace and leadership."

He was more than ready, so together — sitting in my car in the parking lot outside Schlotzsky's Deli — we prayed and Steve asked Jesus to be his Savior and Lord.

It was an amazing moment. You might wonder how to celebrate after something like this. We wondered the same thing, but while we were considering the question, we hurried in and had sandwiches.

As we drove back to the church, I prayed again out loud, asking God to give Steve the assurance that he was now God's son and that he would be filled with joy. He later told me that as I spoke he kept praying, "Yes, Lord Jesus." He said that "suddenly the word *Lord* took on a whole new meaning. It was as if the four letters of that word radiated with red and blue and gold colors. I kept saying, 'LORD Jesus' — just those two words over and over. I finally understood the word *Lord* and I laughed and cried."

This truly was a turning point in Steve's life. Over the years, Steve has grown immensely in his faith, written a couple of devotional books, and even served for a season as the pastor of a church. I only spent about an hour with him that day, but thankfully God gave me the clarity to challenge him with the incisive truths of the gospel. Then I got to watch as God did the rest.

Talk about *adventure*!

> Action Principle

We often get stymied in our outreach efforts because we're convinced we need to be better prepared, know the Bible inside and out, and have answers for every possible question. Often, we forget two things: First, the Holy Spirit is with us, directing and using what we say, and second, God's Word has divine power to cut to the heart and challenge people with the truth about Christ. We should prepare as much as we can but then trust in the guidance of God and the power of his gospel, seizing every opportunity we can.

Stepping into the Adventure ‹ · · · · ·

Nobody wants to offend other people. But telling them God's truth is to risk doing just that: upsetting and possibly insulting them and, in some cases, even jeopardizing your relationship with them. And yet that's the risk we must take in order to tell them what God says and to give his Word the opportunity to show itself to be "living and active. Sharper than any double-edged sword, it penetrates even to dividing soul and spirit, joints and marrow; it judges the thoughts and attitudes of the heart" (Hebrews 4:12).

Similarly, no doctor likes to tell patients that they have a life-threatening disease. Doing so risks patients getting angry, and it might even result in them rejecting medical advice and deciding to find a different physician. Still, it's a situation that no good doctor will try to dodge.

Patients *must* hear the bad news so that they have the opportunity to face the facts and find a remedy. The "cure" might come in the form of better nutrition and exercise, medication, radiation, or surgery, but patients aren't willing to apply those solutions until they believe they really have a problem.

The Bible's message is a mix of bad news and good news. The *bad news* is that we are sinners who break God's laws, fall short of his standards, and therefore deserve his punishment, which is spiritual separation and death for all of eternity. That's the hopeless spiritual predicament we find ourselves in, and we're morally helpless on our own to change it, as the first three chapters of Romans make abundantly clear.

That's really bad news. But when people let those realities sink

> When we lovingly communicate that message to others — the bad *and* the good news — it has power to impact their lives forever.

in, they become much more receptive to the *good news*, which is that Jesus came to pay our penalty for us. He willingly died on the cross to take upon himself the punishment for our sins so that we could trade our sin and shame for his forgiveness, leadership, and eternal life (see Romans 4 – 8).

When we lovingly communicate that message to others — the bad *and* the good news — it has power to impact their lives forever. So as the Holy Spirit opens opportunities for you, don't shrink back from proclaiming God's truth, humbly and clearly. Then watch him work in the lives of your family and friends.

> Inspiration for the Journey

I came to you in weakness and fear, and with much trembling. My message and my preaching were not with wise and persuasive words, but with a demonstration of the Spirit's power, so that your faith might not rest on men's wisdom, but on God's power.

1 Corinthians 2:3 – 5

THOSE ODD COINCIDENCES

LEE STROBEL

What emotions would you feel if you suddenly found yourself standing before an audience of more than a thousand skeptics, seekers, and Christians — all of whom had been told that they can pepper you for ninety minutes with absolutely any question about God, Jesus, the Bible, world religions, or any other spiritual topic?

Uh-huh. Exactly. That's how *I* felt: apprehensive ... nervous ... *scared.* I had never done this before. Granted, I did have one comfort: I would be fielding questions alongside my ministry partner Mark Mittelberg, one of the smartest guys I know, so that ratcheted up my confidence a bit. However, I had underestimated another presence that would end up making all the difference in the world.

The chances are you will never invite a crowd to pummel you with spiritual objections. Nevertheless, read on. There's a lesson for both you and me in the story of an amazing "coincidence" that exposed God's clandestine activity, the kind of divine intervention that makes me grateful I didn't miss this episode of the unexpected adventure of faith.

The question-and-answer event was scheduled for a Sunday evening in Atlanta. At noon that day, Mark and I were eating lunch when we happened to get into a conversation with a highly opinionated skeptic who raised an objection to Christianity that I had never considered before.

"There was a mythological god named Mithras, worshiped long before Jesus, who was born of a virgin on December 25, was a great traveling teacher, sacrificed himself for world peace, and was resurrected from the dead after three days in a tomb," he claimed. "You see, Christianity merely copied its beliefs from a myth."

This allegation has become much more prevalent in recent years, especially after the publication of *The Da Vinci Code*, but back then this was new stuff to me. Nobody had ever leveled that charge in any conversation with me before that day. I stumbled around trying to give him an answer, but unfortunately I did a lot more stumbling than answering.

> I felt a strong impression that God was using this lunchtime encounter to prepare me.

Back at the hotel, as Mark and I were getting ready and praying for the event, I felt a strong impression that God was using this lunchtime encounter to prepare me. I sensed that he was prodding me to get ready with an answer because in his divine foreknowledge he was aware that a seeker was going to be asking that very question.

So I spent the next several hours focused on the Mithras issue. I called an expert on the topic and scoured scholarly articles. As I suspected, the plagiarism charge was grossly inaccurate. According to the actual myth, Mithras wasn't born of a virgin but supposedly emerged fully grown from a rock; he wasn't a traveling teacher but a mythological god; he didn't sacrifice himself but instead was famous for slaying a bull; and there were no beliefs about his death and hence no resurrection. As for being born December 25 — well, so what? The Bible doesn't tell us what day Jesus was born. Besides, Mithraism didn't even emerge as a mystery religion until *after* Christianity was already established.

I went to the event that evening anxious to unload all the facts I had researched. Despite my initial nervousness, the whole evening worked out well. People asked sincere questions on a wide range of topics, and by God's grace Mark and I were able to address their issues. The whole time, though, I kept waiting in eager anticipation for the Mithras objection to be raised. Yet the question never came.

I was puzzled. The impression in my spirit had been so strong that God wanted me to get ready to deal with this issue. *That's really odd*, I mused as we left the venue. *I guess I was misreading things.*

I promptly forgot about the incident until two weeks later when Mark and I were standing in front of three hundred seekers and skeptics at a church in Chicago. After about an hour of answering questions, I glanced at my watch and saw it was time for us to finish. When I looked up, though, I noticed a young man in the front row with his hand raised.

"Okay, one last question," I said, gesturing toward him.

He cleared his throat as he stood. "Isn't it true," he began, sounding challenging in his tone, "that Christianity actually plagiarized its beliefs from people who worshiped the mythical god Mithras?"

Mark couldn't help but smile. "That's a really good question," he said. "Lee, I think you should address this one."

With that, I launched into a lengthy explanation for why this claim totally lacks merit, giving detail after detail that I had gleaned from my recent studies in Atlanta. Because God had prompted me to investigate the topic, I was able to offer a thorough and persuasive rebuttal to what was at the time an obscure objection.

As I spoke, I could see the defensiveness dissolve from the young man's demeanor. He appeared to become increasingly receptive to my answer. When I finished, I asked him, "Do you have any further questions about that?"

"Uh, no," he said. Then as he was sitting down, I heard him say, partly to himself, partly to me, partly to the woman sitting next to him, and I think partly to the Lord: "That was the last barrier between me and God."

The last barrier. And before the night was over, he prayed to receive Christ as his forgiver and leader.

Was that a coincidence? I don't think so. The Mithras objection wouldn't gain widespread popularity for several more years. The fact that it was raised in Atlanta in an impromptu discussion, that I felt God distinctly leading me to get ready with an answer, and that it was raised in front of hundreds of people just a couple of weeks later and helped bring down the last barrier between this guy and God — no, to me, that's more than mere happenstance.

Rather, it was one more reminder that evangelism is never a solo activity. God is always working behind the scenes to draw people to himself. And one of the greatest thrills in sharing our faith is to catch occasional glimpses of his covert activity. It's almost as if he's winking at us and saying, *You ain't seen nothin' yet. Stick with me and I'll show you some "divine coincidences" that will rock your world and exponentially expand your faith.*

> Evangelism is never a solo activity. God is always working behind the scenes to draw people to himself.

Action Principle ◄ ······

If you want to increase your own faith, then share your faith with others. As you do, you'll be playing a role in the great redemptive drama that God is unfolding around the globe. From time to time, as a partner in his Great Commission, you'll be able to witness firsthand how the Holy Spirit is orchestrating events, encounters, and conversations in amazing and inspiring ways. And as a result, you will walk away with a stronger and more vibrant faith of your own.

Stepping into the Adventure ◄ ······

In their classic book *Experiencing God*, Henry Blackaby and Claude King encourage Christians to find out where God is already at work and then to join him in it. When we do that, they said, we will experience the greatest adventure and thrills of the Christian life.

The Bible tells us with great clarity that there's no activity more urgent to God than reconciling people to himself. That's the reason Jesus entered into the fray of humanity: "to seek and to save what was lost" (Luke 19:10). It's the assignment he gave the church in the Great Commission when he told us to "go and make disciples of all nations" (see Matthew 28:19 – 20). He's even holding back the consummation of history in order for more and more people to find redemption and eternal life (2 Peter 3:9).

When we join God in this supremely important undertaking, we can be sure that we're within his will. Therefore we can anticipate that we will experience God in new ways as we work in tandem with him and watch him unleash his supernatural powers to help us in our task.

I've seen it time and time again. For instance, one college student told me he had been drunk all night on Florida's Gulf Coast during spring break. At dawn, he was having deep regrets about the kind of life he was living. He wanted to find God, yet there were many intellectual obstacles in his way. *How can there be a loving God if there's so much suffering in the world? How can a loving God send people to hell? How can Jesus be the only way to heaven?*

He was pondering these objections as he strolled down the deserted beach. Then suddenly he saw something half buried in the sand right in front of him. "If I had walked a little to the left or a little to the right, I wouldn't have seen it," he told me.

But there it was so squarely in his path that he almost tripped over it: a well-worn copy of my book *The Case for Faith*, in which I provide answers to the precise barriers that were keeping this young man from faith. He dug out the book, wiped off the sand, read it — and ended up committing his life to Christ.

"I have no idea why the book was there," he told me.

Well, I do. It was there because God is the Great Evangelist who loves him more than anyone on earth ever could. Several years earlier, when God's Spirit prodded me to write that book, I'm sure that young man's eternity was on God's mind. Putting the book right in his path — well, that's child's play for the One whose voice called the very universe into existence.

> Inspiration for the Journey

Come and see what God has done, his awesome deeds for humankind!

Psalm 66:5 TNIV

A TIME FOR URGENCY

MARK MITTELBERG

I hadn't seen my great uncle in years, and I knew I would probably never see him again. He was getting up in age and suffering from a serious illness. Everyone in the family knew he was near the end of his life, which made his upcoming visit to my parents' home all the more poignant — and important.

As children, my siblings and I loved going out of town to "Aunt Faye and Uncle Maurice's house." Part of the attraction was their fascinating home itself. It was one of those old-fashioned places that through the years had become a veritable storehouse of unusual trinkets and toys. To our delight, Aunt Faye would send us kids upstairs with the encouragement to have fun rummaging around and seeing what interesting things we could find to play with. We enthusiastically took her up on her offer, sometimes for hours on end.

> I hadn't seen my great uncle in years, and I knew I would probably never see him again.

Maurice was always warm and jovial, and, thinking back, Faye was sort of like our very own Aunt Bee (of *The Andy Griffith*

Show), always concerning herself with meals for her visitors and treats for us kids. *What's not to like about this?* I used to think.

It wasn't until years later that I learned some of the grown-ups were concerned about Uncle Maurice's spiritual condition. A vaguely religious man, he had occasionally attended church but seemed to view it mostly as a place of social interaction and influence, not a source of spiritual life and transformation. What's worse, he sometimes overtly denied the need to ask for Jesus' forgiveness and leadership in his life. It was my growing awareness of these things as a young Christian that made me extra prayerful as his visit approached.

Though struggling with his health when he arrived, Maurice was his usual good-natured self. We enjoyed our time with him, sharing meals and talking by the fireplace as we reminisced about "the good old days," including memories of Aunt Faye, who had died several years earlier.

But I also had a gnawing sense that God was leading me to talk with him about the importance of knowing and following Christ while he still had the opportunity to do so. I struggled with this, as Maurice was more than fifty years my senior. *Who was I to tell this older and more experienced man what he should do?* I thought. *Surely there must be someone else in the family better equipped to talk to him.* Yet I couldn't shake the feeling that God wanted me to speak up.

Finally, after Maurice had been with us for several days and was nearing the end of his visit, I knew I couldn't put the conversation off any longer. He was sitting on an upholstered chair that was opposite a matching one, with an ottoman in between. I sat on the chair across from him and told him I had something important to talk about.

Perhaps detecting my nervousness, he cordially asked me what I wanted to discuss. I took a deep breath and told him of my spiritual concerns for him. I explained how just a few years earlier, I had fully trusted in Christ myself. I talked about how God had begun changing me from the inside out and had given me a new sense of security and hope. I told him I wanted him to have that same security and hope.

Maurice smiled and gently told me I needn't worry about him. He was confident that God was kind and loving, and that he would be okay when the day came for him to pass on.

"How do you *know* you'll be okay?" I asked him.

"Well, I've lived a pretty good life," he insisted, "and I think God will see that and be fair to me."

"But that's not how it works," I responded. "The Bible makes it clear that none of us is good enough or has done enough good works to earn God's forgiveness. It says in Romans 3:23 that we all have sinned and fallen short of God's standard. That's why Jesus had to die — to pay the penalty for these sins we've each committed."

Again he tried to brush off my concerns, assuring me that he would be all right and that he had nothing to fear.

The best way I can describe what happened next is that I suddenly realized it was now or never, and a kind of holy boldness came over me. I slid from my chair onto the ottoman between us. Sitting directly in front of him, I took hold of his hands and looked straight into his eyes.

"Uncle Maurice," I said, "I love you enough to tell you the truth. It's only a matter of weeks or months or, at the very most, a few short years before you'll literally stand in front of Jesus, and he is going to ask you whether you trusted in him and accepted his payment for your sins. He's already told us that we're sinners in desperate need of his salvation and that he is the only way to God, so please don't turn away from him and his offer of forgiveness and life."

Maurice thanked me for caring so deeply. I think he was touched by my love and concern, but he showed no outward signs of spiritual softening. A few days later he left and I never saw him again. I did, however, follow up a few months later with a letter that again emphatically expressed my concerns and retold the message of the gospel.

Recently I was going through some old files and found a photocopy of that letter. Here is part of what it said:

Dear Uncle Maurice,

I'm really glad that you were able to come stay with us last fall. I enjoyed spending time with you. You're a very kind and dear man, and I'm happy to have you as my "Uncle."

I love you, and because I love you, I have to tell you that I'm deeply troubled and concerned for you, in more than the physical sense. I'm concerned about your relationship to God, and whether or not you are his child. I know we talked about it when you were here. But talking about it is not enough. You must respond...."

I never received a reply. A few years later we got the report that Maurice had died. We were all sad to hear the news, and I realized that I would never know this side of eternity how he had responded to what I had said.

But I also sensed God's quiet affirmation, assuring me that my efforts had honored and pleased him. I had done everything I could to communicate the gospel clearly, to stress the urgency of the situation, and to commit it all to God in prayer. I knew ultimately that's all we can do — and then leave the results in his strong and loving hands.

Action Principle

The evangelistic journey is full of excitement and adventure, but it is also *serious*. We're not merely try-ing to help people improve their lives. We're pointing them to Jesus, who unambiguously declared, "I am the way and the truth and the life. No one comes to the Father except through me" (John 14:6). We need to cultivate the courage to speak up and lovingly explain the gospel to people — sometimes with great urgency.

> We need to cultivate the courage to speak up and lovingly explain the gospel to people — sometimes with great urgency.

Stepping into the Adventure

One of the most sobering passages in the Bible is found in Ezekiel 3 where, beginning in verse 17, God says, "Son of man, I have made you a watchman for the house of Israel; so hear the word I speak and give them warning from me." Then he proceeds to explain that if Ezekiel is faithful to sound the warning clearly, then the responsibility will fall upon the people to heed it. But if he doesn't warn them clearly, that responsibility will fall back on Ezekiel. Needless to say, Ezekiel takes this very seriously, making sure he conveys whatever God tells him to say to the people he is called to confront.

Similarly, each of us is a member of the church to which Jesus gave the command to go into the world and communicate his gospel. This message is good news, but it's built on the sober-ing reality that we are all sinners in need of a Savior. We must communicate clearly the truth about our sin and the punishment we deserve, as well as the great news that our penalty has been paid by Jesus, who offers forgiveness and new life as a gift of his grace.

I sought to convey this to Uncle Maurice. Looking back, I don't know whether I hit the right balance between patience and persistence. But I'll tell you this: I've always been thankful that in that situation I leaned more toward persistence and didn't hold back. It felt a bit risky, and I was a little uncomfortable. But I had nothing to lose, and my great-uncle had everything to gain. What Maurice ultimately did with the message was his responsibility. But I know in my heart that I spoke the truth clearly, motivated by love.

Ask God to give you the proper balance in your own interactions with family and friends. Be patient but also persistent, and be willing to challenge people with intensity and urgency as the Holy Spirit leads.

Inspiration for the Journey

Be merciful to those who doubt; snatch others from the fire and save them; to others show mercy, mixed with fear.

Jude 1:22 – 23

HANG TIME

LEE STROBEL

I pulled up to my friend's house in a tiny convertible sports car. "You want us to drive across the country in *that*?" he said with a laugh.

"What do you mean?" I replied, feigning indignation. "Leslie and I drove all the way from Illinois to Florida in it last year."

He looked incredulous. "On *purpose*?"

Soon we were bantering like old times. Tarik and I had met as students at the University of Missouri, and on weekends we hitchhiked across the prairie to check out custom motorcycle shops in Joplin and Kansas City. Our wanderlust continued after we graduated, including a trip down to New Orleans during the Super Bowl to explore Bourbon Street and the rowdy football parties going on before and after the event. But now we were about to embark on an adventure with more serious overtones.

Because Tarik was working in Iowa and I lived in Chicago, we hadn't seen each other for several years. However, I heard vague rumors that he was facing some personal opportunities and challenges, and I doubted whether he had anyone he could trust to talk to about them. Besides, we had never really discussed my newfound faith in Christ.

So I called and said, "Hey, remember those road trips we used to go on? Let's take a week off from work and drive."

Surprisingly, Tarik didn't need any convincing. "All right. Why not? Pick me up."

He didn't ask what I would be driving, hence his dismay when I showed up in a blue Mazda Miata with the top down. The car barely seats two, but he squeezed inside and off we headed west without any particular destination in mind.

I don't think we turned on the radio the whole way. We just talked and talked. Actually, my role for the first couple of days was simply to listen. He was troubled about some impending deci- sions, and so for hours on end he discussed them in depth. I offered advice whenever I could.

Before long, we hit Omaha, had a nice steak dinner, and then decided to turn south. In Kansas, driving down U.S. Highway 281, we stumbled upon the geographical center of the forty-eight states, marked by a small monument and a tiny chapel that might seat six people. We ventured inside, where I pretended to preach a sermon; Tarik, raised in a Muslim home, didn't look very com- fortable in the wooden pew.

Soon after that we were zipping down Highway 24 through Cawker City, Kansas, when I slammed on the brakes, put the car in reverse, and backed up to confirm what I thought I had seen. Sure enough, it was the World's Biggest Ball of Twine, all seven million feet of it, coiled into a ball approaching ten feet in diam- eter and enshrined in a large gazebo. Not quite awe-inspiring, but certainly worth a couple of campy photos.

As we approached Kansas City, our conversation turned to faith. The thorny challenges he was facing, I said to Tarik, might be less daunting if he had the comfort, wisdom, and guidance of Christ in his life.

Having been born in an Islamic country, Tarik was culturally Muslim, but he wasn't actively devout. When we were in college, the topic of religion came up only once, when we got into a disagreement about God. Tarik was aghast that I *didn't* believe in him, while I was astounded that he *did*.

As we drove, I told him the story of how I investigated the evidence for Jesus, and I described the way my new faith had changed my worldview, attitudes, and priorities. We stopped in Kansas City and went to a Royals baseball game that night, chattering about Christianity between innings. The following day we headed down Interstate 70 to Columbia to visit the University of Missouri, where we had met more than twenty years earlier.

We had a great time exploring our old dormitory and hangouts. At the end of the day, I stopped at a Christian bookstore so I could buy a Bible for Tarik. The next morning, before we left the hotel, I said to him, "Let me clarify what Christianity is about." I leafed through the New Testament to Romans 6:23: "For the wages of sin is death, but the gift of God is eternal life in Christ Jesus our Lord."

"That," I said to Tarik, "pretty much sums it up. We deserve death, eternal separation from God, because of our sin or wrongdoing. But God offers us forgiveness and eternal life as a gift, purchased when Jesus died on the cross as our substitute to pay for all of our transgressions." I emphasized the word *gift* to contrast with Muslim teachings, which emphasize doing good works to try to appease Allah.

Tarik listened politely but didn't say much about this. As we headed north toward Iowa, I would bring up the gospel from time to time, but he seemed reluctant to talk about it. I tried not to get discouraged, telling myself that he was probably mulling over the implications of the verse. But deep inside I wondered. His personal challenges were weighing heavily on him. Did he see Jesus as a potential help or as a meaningless diversion?

It was late when we returned to his house. "I've got to leave early in the morning," I said as I was getting ready to head to the guest room. I was going to leave it at that, but I decided to take one more shot.

"Remember, we talked about how the Bible says forgiveness and eternal life are a gift," I said. "Would you like to pray with me to receive that gift? We could do that right here, right now."

His response stunned me. "Yes," he said. "I'd like to do that." And that evening, Tarik prayed with me to make Christ his Savior.

I cranked up the praise music as I drove back to Chicago the following morning. Tarik and I had spent five days meandering around the countryside. We had given up precious vacation time from work in order to spend those days hanging out together. But it was, I mused, a small investment compared to the eternal results.

> Action Principle

Years ago, parenting "experts" said it wasn't the *quantity* of time you spent with your children that was important, it was the *quality* of the time that mattered. Of course, they were wrong: *both* are important. Likewise, many times the best gift we can give our spiritually seeking friends is our time, a listening ear, and a caring heart.

> Many times the best gift we can give our spiritually seeking friends is our time, a listening ear, and a caring heart.

Stepping into the Adventure ← ······

In football, "hang time" refers to how long the pigskin remains aloft after being kicked. In basketball, it's the length of time a player is suspended as he soars through the air to dunk the ball. In the unexpected adventure of evangelism, "hang time" refers to something else: hanging out with your seeking friends long enough to really get to know them, to understand their questions and concerns, to deepen the trust between you, and to allow yourselves to delve deeply into spiritual conversations.

If you're a parent, you know that the best discussions with your children, especially when they are little, don't come in the first few minutes of your interaction with them. They come much later, after you've invested enough time to convince them that you really do care about what's going on in their lives.

Time, after all, is our most precious commodity. When we generously share it with others, we're telling them that they really do matter to us. We're creating an unhurried environment in which there's at least the potential for meaningful discussions about important issues — especially eternal ones.

One of the most moving examples of a Christian investing "hang time" is described by Terry Muck in his book *Those Other Religions in Your Neighborhood*. He recounts a letter written by a man who had lacked any spiritual interest, but who lived next door to a committed Christian.

They had a casual relationship involving talks over the backyard fence, borrowing lawn mowers, stuff like that. Then the non-Christian's wife was stricken with cancer and soon died. Here's part of the letter he wrote afterward:

> I was in total despair. I went through the funeral preparations and the service like I was in a trance. And after the service I went to the path along the river and walked all

night. *But I did not walk alone.* My neighbor — afraid for me, I guess — stayed with me all night.

He did not speak; he did not even walk beside me. He just followed me. When the sun finally came up over the river, he came over to me and said, "Let's go get some breakfast."

I go to church now. My neighbor's church. *A religion that can produce the kind of caring and love my neighbor showed me is something I want to find out more about.* I want to be like that. I want to love and be loved like that for the rest of my life.[21]

What a powerful impact a few hours of walking along a riverfront had on that man. Isn't it interesting how he equates the time his friend spent with him — saying nothing and doing nothing in particular — with "caring and love."

So who do you need some "hang time" with? Maybe it's an acquaintance who is going through a crisis in his life. Or perhaps it's someone from work or your neighborhood with whom you have only a surface-level connection. Spending time with them might foster a new friendship and open the door to spiritual conversations.

It's amazing how one phone call or visit can instantly rekindle a long-ago relationship and set the groundwork for a life-changing encounter.

Or maybe, like my friend Tarik, it's a person you've drifted away from in recent years. It's amazing how one phone call or visit can instantly rekindle a long-ago relationship and set the groundwork for a life-changing encounter.

Inspiration for the Journey

We are therefore Christ's ambassadors, as though God were making his appeal through us.

2 Corinthians 5:20

RIPPLE EFFECTS

MARK MITTELBERG

Wende was a high-flying corporate type, reached by God through a variety of influences, including Christian friends, an evangelistic church, a leader who took the time to challenge her, and a copy of *The Journey: A Bible for the Spiritually Curious.* Wende's curiosity and God's grace soon led her into a committed walk with Christ.

Suddenly this opened a whole new world for Wende as she realized that many of her coworkers, friends, and even family members needed God's love, forgiveness, and guidance — and that he wanted to use her to reach them. As a result, even in the earliest stages of Wende's spiritual development, she began to take everyday risks to communicate her newfound faith to the people around her. I met Wende during that time and had the privilege of becoming an informal coach and occasional partner in some of those outreach efforts.

One of the first people she helped bring to Christ was her son. At a very early age, TJ began to understand, largely through the changes he saw in his mom, that God is real, loves him, and wants to be his forgiver and closest friend.

It wasn't long after this that the pastor of our church introduced Wende to an Asian businesswoman he had invited to our weekend services, someone he thought Wende might be able to help in her spiritual journey. Because of their similar corporate backgrounds, they had a natural affinity and began to have frequent discussions about a variety of topics, including faith. Soon Wende had the opportunity to lead her in a prayer of commitment to Christ, which only fueled Wende's passion to reach out more.

> As Wende's spiritual discernment grew, she became aware that her own father, although a faithful church attender, probably didn't have an authentic relationship with Christ.

As Wende's spiritual discernment grew, she became aware that her own father, although a faithful church attender, probably didn't have an authentic relationship with Christ. So she began having conversations with him about it on the phone and whenever they could get together.

Wende and I discussed Bob's situation often. A strong personality and a hard-hitting leader, her dad was a bit of a character too. He had recently purchased and was remodeling a ranch in a remote part of Colorado. He loved to drive on the mountainous back roads in his four-wheel-drive truck, always carrying firearms "just in case anything happens."

I was amused by her descriptions of him and figured he was the kind of colorful person I'd get along with just fine. I told her that the next time he came to the area, we should all have a meal together so we could discuss spiritual matters.

Before long, Bob scheduled a trip to Chicago, and Wende was able to line up a breakfast meeting. Wende, TJ, Bob, and I met at my favorite pancake house. I figured that even if the conversation went poorly, I would at least enjoy some good food before Bob decided to shoot me.

We had a great meal and an invigorating conversation regarding several questions Bob had jotted down while reading some books Wende had sent him. After talking about random spiritual topics for a while, I sensed it might clarify the issues if I could present a more complete picture of the gospel message.

I got out a pen, turned over a paper placemat (the one without syrup on it), and drew the bridge illustration the same way we teach it in the *Becoming a Contagious Christian* training course. It's a simple but eye-opening aid to understanding that God is on one side of a chasm and we're on the other, separated by our disobedience and sin and unable to do anything to earn, bargain, or buy our way back to him. It shows graphically that all of our efforts fall short and that the penalty we deserve is death, which is spiritual separation from God.

I drew the diagram for Bob, carefully explaining each part, especially the last point when I drew the cross of Christ that alone forms the bridge by which we can get over the chasm to God. I presented it in the hope that Bob would be open to hearing this sobering biblical message. He was not only open, God had so prepared his heart that he quickly affirmed its truth and indicated that he wanted to step across the chasm to God's side.

I wanted to lead Bob in a prayer of commitment right away, but I didn't think the bustling restaurant was a good place to do so. Instead, I suggested that we continue the discussion out in Bob's rental car, which would provide the privacy we needed. And that's what we did. Bob sat in the driver's seat, I was in the passenger seat, and Wende and TJ were in the back.

After a little more discussion, Bob was ready to pray to receive salvation. It was quite a moment when he, Wende, and I joined hands in the middle of the car and — just as we were about to pray together — tiny TJ put his pudgy little hand on top of ours and watched as his grandfather asked Jesus to be his forgiver and leader.

It's hard to put into words the meaning and impact of experiences like this, but suffice it to say there's nothing on the planet as exciting or rewarding as the adventure of leading someone in a prayer of commitment to Christ.

The adventure didn't stop there. Soon Bob and Wende teamed up as a father-daughter evangelistic duo to reach out to a dying relative on the East Coast. I should have warned "Uncle Lynn" to just give up when he saw these two coming because, sure enough, he soon became a follower of Jesus as well, only a couple of weeks before he died.

Since then, Wende and I have moved to different parts of the country. Nevertheless, I had the privilege of partnering with her again as she and her husband led a citywide outreach campaign in their city, through which many thousands heard the gospel and a great number of people made commitments to Christ.

> When you're weighing whether to take a risk to tell others about Jesus, it's motivating to remember that you might ultimately impact many others through them.

Today Bob is involved in helping several ministries in Colorado. He is also a seasoned elder of his church, occasionally even preaching the Sunday sermon. So the impact continues to spread and will go on, person to person to person, rippling down through the corridors of time and all the way into eternity.

⟩ Action Principle

When you're weighing whether to take a risk to tell others about Jesus, it's motivating to remember that you might ultimately impact many others through them. As in Wende's case, one person might go on to reach a child, a friend, a parent, an uncle, and perhaps a significant part of a community for Christ. Your limited efforts could have a ripple effect down through history, even touching limitless numbers of lives throughout future generations.

Stepping into the Adventure

By today's standards, Jesus didn't speak to huge numbers of people. Occasionally he taught moderately large crowds but never the size of audiences that Billy Graham, for example, spoke to for decades. The number was certainly far fewer than can be touched simultaneously through today's media. Mostly Jesus spoke to a tight circle of friends and to small gatherings of people who crowded around to hear what he had to say. And relatively few of them became his followers.

Yet Jesus changed the world.

How did he have such an incredible impact? He understood the ripple effect he would have by reaching even a limited number of men and women, helping them become dedicated disciples and then challenging them to get in on the adventure of bringing his love and truth to as many others as possible. He knew that some would reach only a handful, while others would shake entire nations. The collective long-term influence would be enormous.

Where do you fit in? How do you put yourself into the flow of God's plan to touch the world? *Just reach out to another person.* You don't have to speak to hoards of people, start a media ministry, or write the next Christian blockbuster. If God calls you to do those things, great. But most of us are called to share God's message with just a few people around us: our own kids. The neighbors down the block. The gas station attendant. A waiter or waitress. The person behind the counter at the dry cleaners. Colleagues at work. Your Uncle Frank or Aunt Helen. Mom or Dad. A niece or nephew. The overnight delivery man. The student with the locker across the hall from yours. The children in a Sunday school class.

Get a vision for who those people are, how much they matter to God, and the magnitude of what God might do in and through them. The young woman you reach might end up being the next Wende. The scrawny young boy you lead to faith might become the next Billy Graham. Reach out to the people in your world who are now within reach and trust God for his amazing long-term results.

> Inspiration for the Journey

Remember this: Whoever sows sparingly will also reap sparingly, and whoever sows generously will also reap generously.

2 Corinthians 9:6

ADDICTED TO LIFE CHANGE

LEE STROBEL

All right, I'll admit it: I'm an addict. I crave stories of how God has revolutionized the lives of once wayward people.

Like the story of Billy Moore, who confessed to murdering an elderly man during a robbery. Before being sentenced to Death Row, Billy was visited by two Christians who explained that forgiveness and hope are available through Christ. "Nobody ever told me that Jesus loves me and died for me," Billy said. "It was a love I could feel. It was a love I wanted. It was a love I *needed.*"

> I crave stories of how God has revolutionized the lives of once wayward people.

Billy was baptized in a bathtub outside his cell, and God began to change him from the inside out. He took dozens of Bible courses by correspondence and began counseling other inmates and even troubled teenagers sent to him by local churches. For sixteen years, he was a humble missionary inside the prison, "a saintly figure" in the words of the *Atlanta Journal and Constitution.*

In fact, he became so thoroughly transformed that the Georgia Parole and Pardon Board ended up doing something unprecedented: they actually opened the gates of Death Row and set him free. Today he's an ordained minister, a man of compassion and prayer who spends his time helping people who are hurting and forgotten.

When I visited Billy in his home, I asked about the source of his amazing metamorphosis. "It was the prison rehabilitation system, right?" I asked.

Moore laughed. "No, it wasn't that."

"Then it was a self-help program or having a positive mental attitude," I suggested.

He shook his head emphatically. "No, not that, either."

"Prozac? Transcendental Meditation? Psychological counseling?"

"Come on, Lee," he said. "You know it wasn't any of those."

He was right. I knew the real reason. I just wanted to hear him say it.

"Plain and simple, it was Jesus Christ," he declared adamantly. "He changed me in ways I could never have changed on my own. He gave me a reason to live. He helped me do the right thing. He gave me a heart for others. He saved my soul."

Stories like that fire me up. Go ahead, admit it: you're just as passionate as I am about witnessing how God redeems and then redeploys the most improbable characters — even people like you and me.

I saw it again in the life of Robert. He got his thrills from dramatically cheating death. His life was awash in booze and one willing woman after another. He made piles of money and gambled much of it away. He once used a baseball bat to settle a dispute with an associate, which landed him in jail.

He was the quintessential narcissist. At the height of his success, he owned two private jets that cost thousands of dollars an hour to operate. One day he ordered both of them into the air. The reason? He wanted to sit inside one of them, sipping expensive champagne, while he looked out the window at the other one flying in tandem — just so he could see his name emblazoned on its tail as it soared through the sky.

Robert didn't hate God; in a way, it was worse than that. At least despising God would have required emotion. Instead, God was simply irrelevant to him. Unneeded. A nonissue.

Until one day when the most extraordinary thing happened: God spoke to him. Not out loud, but internally. He could actually sense God saying, "Robert, I've rescued you more times than you'll ever know. Now I want you to come to me through my Son Jesus."

Robert was shocked. Why was God speaking to him out of the blue? And who is Jesus really? He wasn't at all sure. He called a friend who was a Christian and started asking him questions. The friend suggested he get my book *The Case for Christ*, which he ended up reading cover to cover. God reached Robert through that book, through the prayers of his daughter and her church, and most powerfully by the direct touch of his Spirit.

"All of a sudden, I just believed in Jesus Christ. I did! I believed in him!" Robert declared with wide-eyed enthusiasm. "I just got on my knees and prayed that God would put his arms around me and never, ever, ever let me go."

Starting at that moment, Robert began to change in ways that only the Holy Spirit can accomplish. His hardened shell softened. His selfishness began to dissolve. His priorities were turned upside down. Suddenly he couldn't do enough for God. He became as passionate about his relationship with Christ as anyone I have ever encountered.

When Robert was baptized, he told his story with such simplicity, such emotion, and such childlike conviction that there wasn't a dry eye in the sanctuary. One by one, God began stirring in the hearts of other people that morning. Throughout the church, God was whispering, *Now is the time for you too.*

When the pastor asked if anyone else wanted to receive Christ and be baptized, men and women, young and old, began streaming toward the platform. First ten, then twenty, then a hundred, then two hundred, then three hundred—a total of about *seven hundred* people came forward in two services while the song "Amazing Grace" played.

Amazing grace, indeed.

I became friends with Robert after he called to thank me for writing my book. Since we lived on opposite coasts, we would chat over the phone, usually every other week or so. He was constantly asking questions, always eager to learn more about God and the Bible. His biggest regret, he said, was that he didn't surrender his life to Jesus when he was much younger.

"There's just so much I want to do for him," he told me again and again.

Time, however, was running out. A few months later, Robert died from a lung condition that had plagued him for years. When they buried him near his childhood home in Montana, thousands of people flocked to his funeral to pay tribute to him.

But Robert's last tribute went elsewhere. This unlikely Christian named Robert "Evel" Knievel—the world-famous daredevil motorcyclist who became humbled and awed by God's undeserved love—asked for these words to be etched on his tombstone for all the world to see: "Believe in Jesus Christ."

Please, God, never let me lose my addiction to stories like that.

The most powerful reason for jumping into the unexpected adventure of evangelism is because *people matter to God*, and therefore they should matter to us.

Action Principle ‹ ·····

What motivates you to share Christ with others? Is it a dry sense of guilt or obligation? Or is it a heartfelt desire to see lives transformed and eternities redirected? The most powerful reason for jumping into the unexpected adventure of evangelism is because *people matter to God*, and therefore they should matter to us. When this is the fuel we run on, our evangelistic fires burn brightly.

Stepping into the Adventure ‹ ·····

Sometimes our motivation for talking with others about Christ starts to wane. It can even happen to church leaders. According to a 2005 survey by Christian researcher Thom Rainer, "Over half of pastors have made no evangelistic efforts at all in the past six months. They have not shared the gospel. They have not attempted to engage a lost and unchurched person at any level."[22] When that kind of malaise drags us down — as it does for me, Mark Mittelberg, and every other Christian from time to time — there are practical steps we can take to rejuvenate our passion for helping people find Christ.

First, we can pray, admitting our heart has grown cold and asking God to renew our fire for people who are far from him. As James 4:2 says, "You do not have, because you do not ask God."

Second, we can hang around people whose passion for outreach is contagious. Nothing fires up my enthusiasm like having lunch with Mark and hearing stories of his colorful forays into evangelism. He often says that I have that effect on him as well. Who can you get together with to jump-start your fervor for sharing your faith?

Third, we can read — and reread — biblical passages that teach about God's concerned heart for spiritually confused people. When I return to the story of the prodigal son in Luke 15 or the account of Jesus' encounter with the Samaritan woman in John 4, I always walk away with my heart better synced with God's.

And fourth, we can reflect on the transformed lives we have seen through the years. For instance, I remember one of the most down-and-out individuals I have ever encountered, who approached me for prayer one day after I had spoken at a church.

He was unemployed and broke, his wife had left him, he was on the verge of being evicted, and he was an alcoholic who had attempted suicide. He was unshaven, his hair was long and straggly. Having hit rock bottom, all he could do that day was look up to Christ.

When that same man came up to me two months later, I honestly didn't recognize him. He was clean shaven, well groomed, and nicely dressed. He was sober, employed, and full of hope and optimism. Christ had infused him with fresh purpose; Christians had come to his rescue with practical help. He was there at the church that day so he could gratefully worship and praise the God of the second chance.

"I have a new life," was all he could say as he pumped my hand, tears in his eyes. "I have a new life!"

Stories like those are the lifeblood of the unexpected adventure. They build our faith by reminding us once again that God is *still* in the people transformation business. And who wouldn't want to be a partner in that?

Inspiration for the Journey

Therefore, if anyone is in Christ, he is a new creation; the old has gone, the new has come! All this is from God, who reconciled us to himself through Christ and gave us the ministry of reconciliation.

2 Corinthians 5:17 – 18

RISKS AND REWARDS

MARK MITTELBERG

Do we really have to knock on that door, or can we just stand here for the rest of our lives and avoid this situation?

Neither Lee nor I actually voiced that question, but we both felt it as we stood outside the house gathering our thoughts — and our courage — before announcing our arrival. We knew this would be a rare chance for spiritual impact. Yet sometimes the greater the magnitude of an opportunity, the stronger the force that holds us back from taking action.

Our journey to this doorstep began when the girlfriend of one of the most famous athletes in the world told us she had become a Christian after reading Lee's book *The Case for Christ*. Would the two of us be willing, she asked, to come to her home and talk about Jesus with her boyfriend — who just happens to be a renowned sports icon?

Oh, and did I mention he's a longtime hero of ours? And that he's really smart? And a Muslim who reads the Qur'an in its original Arabic? And not particularly fond of people trying to "proselytize" him?

Oh, boy!

This was one ball we didn't want to fumble. So after a moment's pause at the door, as Lee and I mustered all of the boldness and bravery of two veteran apologists … well, *we paused again.*

So much was riding on this meeting. Were we conversant enough with all of the ins and outs of Islam to have a credible conversation with him? Would we be able to overcome his long-established resistance to the Christian message? We could feel the ripples of apprehension inside of us. Pretty soon, they were waves. *Big* waves.

> Virtually every Christian feels some fear when he or she is about to discuss spiritual matters with someone outside of the faith.

So we said one more prayer, took a deep breath, and quickly rapped on the door before we had the chance to talk ourselves out of the venture completely.

Virtually every Christian feels some fear when he or she is about to discuss spiritual matters with someone outside of the faith. I once asked world-renowned evangelist Luis Palau, who has spoken for decades to millions of people in dozens of countries, whether he ever still gets nervous before talking with someone about Christ. His answer was quick and to the point: "Yes, of course … always."

Oh, good, I thought, *Luis is still human. Yet look at how God uses him. If a guy like him still feels fear, then I guess there's hope for the rest of us.*

We all love the *idea* of adventure, but here's the truth: adventure inevitably involves risk, which in turn always entails some measure of anxiety or nervousness. So if you're feeling apprehensive about an outreach opportunity, it's probably a good sign. It means you're well on your way to experiencing real adventure.

Think about it: anything considered adventurous also contains an element of risk. For instance, I love to ride on my mountain bike, but why? Because I don't just lazily tool around the church parking lot on Saturday afternoons. Instead, I zip through a wilderness area near my house along twisting dirt paths, dodging trees and shrubs and bushes, going around boulders and down steep inclines where there are elements of the unexpected. Sometimes I have to slow down to let a snake slither across the trail. Occasionally I scare up coyotes, encounter poisonous insects, and hear rumors of man-eating mountain lions lurking in the vicinity.

Don't get me wrong: I'm not looking to lurch over a cliff, get bitten by a rattler, or become a hungry cougar's afternoon snack. But the risk of these dangers adds to the sense of the unknown, creating excitement for what otherwise would be a boring and routine bike ride.

Even at amusement parks, we gauge adventure by levels of danger. My kids used to be apprehensive about the kiddie rides. That choo-choo train actually *moves*, so who knows what's going to happen? Those innocuous rides offered just enough fright to make things exciting for them. But appetites for adventure advance with age, and today my teens are taunting *me* to join *them* on Disneyland's Tower of Terror. (So far their recruitment has failed. It's apparent that their desire for *that* kind of excitement has now exceeded their dad's.)

It's interesting that the apostle Paul summed up the biblical understanding of the life of God's people by quoting a verse in the Old Testament and making it part of the New Testament as well: "The righteous will live by faith" (Habakkuk 2:4 and Romans 1:17).

Notice these verses do not say, "The righteous will initially receive salvation by faith, and then they will huddle in safe, predictable, and comfortable places." Rather, we *live* — present tense — by faith.

What is biblical faith? It's "God-directed risk." It's embracing God's unseen salvation, trusting in his unseen protection, obeying his unseen Spirit, following his unseen leadings, building his unseen kingdom, and preparing ourselves and others for his as-of-yet unseen home in heaven. It's the risk of taking him at his word in our daily actions.

It's the phrase Lee quoted in the introduction, about how the Christian life should be "a risky, surprise-filled venture, lived tiptoe at the edge of expectation ... a dancing, leaping, daring life."

So a good paraphrase of these hallmark Old and New Testament verses might be, "The righteous will pursue lives marked by obedient, God-honoring risk taking." When we understand our faith like that, we can quickly see how the Christian life has been architected to be an ongoing and exciting adventure.

We see it in Jesus, where in John 4 he took the risk of hanging out with some Samaritans, starting with the wayward woman at the well. It was a dangerous move in his day of religious and ethnic separatism. He threw caution to the wind and entered another episode in his redemptive adventure, leading to that woman's salvation and the formation of a church among the Samaritan people.

And notice how Jesus hung around so many shady characters: disreputable and despised tax collectors, even prostitutes. In a world stained by sin, Jesus never seemed to meet a sinner he didn't like and in whom he wasn't willing to invest some time. Risky? Of course, that came with the territory. After all, there's always a risk with love.

The ministry of Jesus was attractive and exciting in part because it was filled with God-honoring danger, culminating in his risking everything for the redemption of the world.

I could add the examples of the exhilarating excursions of Paul and the other apostles, the risk-taking leaders of the early church, and the courageous missionaries who have taken the gospel to the ends of the earth, often in settings brimming with trouble and treachery.

These heroes of our faith have set the pattern. The course is laid out, and today's exciting journey is waiting to begin: if you want more adventure in your spiritual life, then you've got to start taking some spiritual risks.

Almost immediately after we knocked, the friend who had invited Lee and me to her home answered the door. Behind her — drinking an iced tea and with body language that screamed, "I don't want these guys *here!*" — stood her famous boyfriend. We walked in with trepidation as she introduced us. He shook our hands but didn't quite look us in the eyes.

Despite that frosty beginning, we soon began to warm to each other. Yes, he was smart and a knowledgeable Muslim. But as we chatted for a while and then sat down to lunch, the tensions diminished. We ended up having a stimulating yet friendly conversation, going back and forth about what Christians and Muslims believe and why.

After several hours, it was like we were old friends. We invited him and his girlfriend to Lee's house for dinner, and they came over a couple of weeks later. Another friend joined us, a former skeptic who had investigated the evidence for Christ, become a Christian, and spent thirty-three years reaching Muslims in Bangladesh. As we grilled steaks in Lee's backyard, we had another spirited and enthusiastic spiritual discussion.

I later continued the conversation with our friend at a downtown coffee shop. As usual, he asked sincere and well-informed questions and raised some formidable challenges but also seemed genuinely interested in the message of Jesus.

While we don't know what might happen as a result of our interactions with him, one thing's for sure: taking the uncomfortable risk to talk to a person like him was flat-out exciting, and we're glad we didn't sidestep or opt out of the opportunity.

As usual, our fear became a portal into the unexpected adventure of the Christian faith.

As usual, our fear became a portal into the unexpected adventure of the Christian faith.

But that's enough about us. We've told our stories, and it's been fun to relive them (well, most of them). Ultimately the unexpected adventure is not about us. It's about what God wants to do through *your life* to reach others.

Whose door is God telling *you* to knock on? What phone call do you need to make, or what email do you know you ought to send? Which neighbor should you invite over for a backyard barbecue? What relative could you reach out to? Who is the old friend you need to reestablish contact with? Ask the Holy Spirit to show you the steps you need to take — big or small — to engage in the unexpected adventure. Then step out and follow his lead *today*.

There's no doubt: it will be a foray into a life of spiritual rewards both in this life and the one yet to come.

MEET THE AUTHORS

Lee Strobel ←

Atheist-turned-Christian Lee Strobel, the former award-winning legal editor of the *Chicago Tribune*, is a *New York Times* best-selling author of more than two dozen books and has been interviewed on numerous national television networks, including ABC, PBS, CNN, and Fox.

Described by the *Washington Post* as "one of the evangelical community's most popular apologists," Lee shared the Christian Book of the Year award in 2005 for a curriculum he coauthored with Garry Poole about *The Passion of the Christ*. He won Gold Medallions for *The Case for Christ, The Case for Faith, The Case for a Creator,* and *Inside the Mind of Unchurched Harry and Mary.* Among his latest books are *The Case for the Real Jesus* and *Finding the Real Jesus.*

Lee was educated at the University of Missouri (bachelor of journalism degree) and Yale Law School (master of studies in law degree). He was a journalist for fourteen years at the *Chicago Tribune* and other newspapers, winning Illinois's top honors for investigative reporting (with a team he led) and public service journalism from United Press International.

A former teaching pastor at two of America's largest churches,

Lee also taught First Amendment law at Roosevelt University. Lee and Leslie have been married for thirty-six years and are the parents of two grown children. Lee's free e-newsletter, "Investigating Faith," is available at *www.LeeStrobel.com*.

> Mark Mittelberg

Mark Mittelberg is a best-selling author, sought-after speaker, and a leading evangelism strategist who has been ministry partners with Lee Strobel for more than twenty years. He is the primary author (along with Strobel and Bill Hybels) of the updated *Becoming a Contagious Christian Training Course*, through which more than a million people around the world have learned to effectively and naturally communicate their faith to others.

Mark is the author of *Choosing Your Faith ... In a World of Spiritual Options*. He also wrote the articles for the accompanying *Choosing Your Faith New Testament*. His other books include *Becoming a Contagious Church*, which sets forth an innovative blueprint for how churches can become mobilized for outreach, and *Becoming a Contagious Christian*, coauthored with Hybels. In addition, Mark was contributing editor for *The Journey: A Bible for the Spiritually Curious* and also contributed to *Reasons for Faith*.

Mark was evangelism director at Willow Creek Community Church in Chicago for seven years and for the Willow Creek Association for a decade. He is a regular speaker for Church Communication Network satellite broadcasts to churches all over North America.

After receiving an undergraduate degree in business, Mark earned a master's degree in philosophy of religion from Trinity Evangelical Divinity School. He lives in Southern California with his wife of twenty-five years, Heidi, and their two teenage children.

SOURCES

1 Eugene H. Peterson, *Traveling Light: Modern Meditations on St. Paul's Letters of Freedom* (Downers Grove, Ill.: InterVarsity, 1988), 45.

2 Immanuel Kant, *Critique of Pure Reason*, trans. Norman Kemp Smith (New York: Palgrave MacMillan, 2003), 65.

3 Alan Loy McGinnis, *Confidence: How to Succeed at Being Yourself* (Minneapolis: Augsburg, 1987), 95.

4 Kerry Shook and Chris Shook, *One Month to Live: Thirty Days to a No-Regrets Life* (Colorado Springs: WaterBrook, 2008), 1.

5 Ibid., 1–2.

6 Frank Newport, "Questions and Answers about Americans' Religion," gallup.com/poll/103459/Questions-Answers-About-Americans-Religion.aspx#3 (Dec. 1, 2008).

7 "Unchurched," Barna.org/FlexPage,aspx?Page=topic&topicID=38 (Dec. 1, 2008).

8 Mark Mittelberg, *Choosing Your Faith … In a World of Spiritual Options* (Wheaton, Ill.: Tyndale, 2008), 17.

9 Charles R. Swindoll, *Come Before Winter and Share My Hope* (Sisters, Ore.: Multnomah, 1985), 43.

10 Ibid.

11 Ibid, 160.

12 Bill Hybels (with LaVonne Neff and Ashley Wiersma), *Too Busy Not to Pray: Slowing Down to Be with God*, 3rd ed. (Downers Grove, Ill.: InterVarsity, 2008), 18.

13 John R. W. Stott, *The Message of the Sermon on the Mount* (Downers Grove, Ill.: InterVarsity, 1993), 119.

[14] Aldous Huxley, *Ends and Means* (London: Chatto & Windus, 1969), 270, 273.

[15] Sheldon Vanauken, *A Severe Mercy* (New York: Harper & Row, 2nd ed., 1980), 85.

[16] Michael Wilkins and J. P. Morelands, eds., *Jesus Under Fire* (Grand Rapids, Mich.: Zondervan, 1996), 144ff.

[17] Georg W. F. Hegel, *Hegel: The Essential Writings* (New York: Harper Perennial, 1977), 15.

[18] Bill Hybels and Mark Mittelberg, *Becoming a Contagious Christian* (Grand Rapids, Mich.: Zondervan, 1996), 64–65.

[19] Lee Strobel, *The Case for Faith: A Journalist Investigates the Toughest Objections to Christianity* (Grand Rapids, Mich.: Zondervan, 2000), 162.

[20] Yancey, Philip, *What's So Amazing About Grace?* (Grand Rapids, Mich.: Zondervan, 2002), 70.

[21] Terry C. Muck, *Those Other Religions in Your Neighborhood: Loving Your Neighbor When You Don't Know How* (Grand Rapids, Mich.: Zondervan, 1992), 150–51, emphasis added.

[22] Thom Rainer, "The Dying American Church," *Baptist Press* (March 28, 2006).

RECOMMENDED RESOURCES

Books on Evangelism

Hybels, Bill. *Just Walk Across the Room*. Grand Rapids, Mich.: Zondervan, 2006.

Hybels, Bill, and Mark Mittelberg. *Becoming a Contagious Christian*. Grand Rapids, Mich.: Zondervan, 1994.

Koukl, Gregory. *Tactics: A Game Plan for Discussing Your Christian Convictions*. Grand Rapids, Mich.: Zondervan, 2008.

Little, Paul. *How to Give Away Your Faith*. Downers Grove, Ill.: InterVarsity, updated edition, 2007.

Mittelberg, Mark. *Becoming a Contagious Church*. Grand Rapids, Mich.: Zondervan, updated edition, 2007.

Pippert, Rebecca Manley. *Out of the Saltshaker and into the World*. Downers Grove, Ill.: InterVarsity, updated edition, 1999.

Poole, Garry. *Seeker Small Groups*. Grand Rapids, Mich.: Zondervan, 2003.

Richardson, Rick. *Evangelism Outside the Box*. Downers Grove, Ill.: InterVarsity, 2000.

Evangelism Training Courses

Hybels, Bill. *Just Walk Across the Room* Curriculum Kit. Grand
Rapids, Mich.: Zondervan, 2006. For small groups.

Mittelberg, Mark, Lee Strobel, and Bill Hybels. *Becoming a
Contagious Christian* Training Course. Grand Rapids, Mich.:
Zondervan, updated DVD edition, 2007. For seminars and small
groups.

Introductory Books to Give Seekers

Lewis, C. S. *Mere Christianity*. New York: HarperOne, 2001.

McDowell, Josh, and Sean McDowell. *More Than a Carpenter*. Carol
Stream, Ill.: Tyndale, updated edition, 2009.

———. *Evidence for the Resurrection*. Ventura, Calif.: Regal, 2008.

Mittelberg, Mark. *Choosing Your Faith ... In a World of Spiritual
Options*. Carol Stream, Ill.: Tyndale, 2008.

Mittelberg, Mark, contributor. *Choosing Your Faith New Testament*.
Carol Stream, Ill.: Tyndale, 2008.

Poling, Judson, and Mark Mittelberg, et al., eds. *The Journey: A Bible
for the Spiritually Curious*. Grand Rapids, Mich.: Zondervan,
1998.

Strobel, Lee. *The Case for Christ*. Grand Rapids, Mich.: Zondervan,
1998. (Also available in student and children editions and on
DVD.)

———. *The Case for Faith*. Grand Rapids, Mich.: Zondervan, 2000.
(Also available in student and children editions and on DVD.)

———. *Finding the Real Jesus*. Grand Rapids, Mich.: Zondervan, 2008.

Warren, Rick. *The Purpose-Driven Life*. Grand Rapids, Mich.:
Zondervan, 2002.

Advanced Books to Give Seekers

Bowman, Robert M. Jr., and J. Ed Komoszewski. *Putting Jesus in His Place: The Case for the Deity of Christ.* Grand Rapids, Mich.: Kregel, 2007.

Craig, William Lane. *Reasonable Faith.* Wheaton, Ill.: Crossway, updated edition, 2008.

Habermas, Gary and Michael Licona, *The Case for the Resurrection of Jesus.* Grand Rapids, Mich.: Kregel, 2004.

Keller, Timothy. *The Reason for God: Belief in an Age of Skepticism.* New York: Dutton, 2008.

Roberts, Mark D. *Can We Trust the Gospels?* Wheaton, Ill.: Crossway, 2007.

Strobel, Lee. *The Case for the Real Jesus.* Grand Rapids, Mich.: Zondervan, 2007. (Also available in student edition.)

———. *The Case for a Creator.* Grand Rapids, Mich.: Zondervan, 2005. (Also available in student and children editions and on DVD.)

Wilkins, Michael J., and J. P. Moreland, eds. *Jesus Under Fire.* Grand Rapids, Mich.: Zondervan, 1996.

DVD-Driven Curricula for Seeker Small Groups

Strobel, Lee, and Garry Poole. *The Case for Christ.* Grand Rapids, Mich.: Zondervan, 2008.

———. *The Case for Faith.* Grand Rapids, Mich.: Zondervan, 2009.

———. *The Case for a Creator.* Grand Rapids, Mich.: Zondervan, 2008.

———. *Faith Under Fire* (4 volumes). Grand Rapids, Mich.: Zondervan, 2006.

———. *Discussing the DaVinci Code.* Grand Rapids, Mich.: Zondervan, 2006.

Study Guides for Seeker Small Groups

Ashton, Mark. *Reality Check* (multiple volumes). Grand Rapids, Mich.: Zondervan, 2002.

Poole, Garry, and Judson Poling. *Tough Questions* (multiple volumes). Grand Rapids, Mich.: Zondervan, 2003.

Richardson, Rick, and Daniel Hill. *Groups Investigating God* (multiple volumes). Downers Grove, Ill.: InterVarsity, 2002.

WILLOW
Willow Creek Association

Willow Creek Association
Vision, Training, Resources for Prevailing Churches

This resource was created to serve you and to help you build a local church that prevails. It is just one of many ministry tools that are part of the Willow Creek Resources® line, published by the Willow Creek Association together with Zondervan.

The Willow Creek Association (WCA) was created in 1992 to serve a rapidly growing number of churches from across the denominational spectrum that are committed to helping unchurched people become fully devoted followers of Christ. Membership in the WCA now numbers over 12,000 Member Churches worldwide from more than ninety denominations.

The Willow Creek Association links like-minded Christian leaders with each other and with strategic vision, training, and resources in order to help them build prevailing churches designed to reach their redemptive potential. Here are some of the ways the WCA does that.

- **The Leadership Summit**—a once a year, two-and-a-half-day conference to envision and equip Christians with leadership gifts and responsibilities. Presented live at Willow Creek as well as via satellite broadcast to over 130 locations across North America, this event is designed to increase the leadership effectiveness of pastors, ministry staff, volunteer church leaders, and Christians in the marketplace.

- **Ministry-Specific Conferences**—throughout each year the WCA hosts a variety of conferences and training events—both at Willow Creek's main campus and offsite, across the U.S., and around the world—targeting church leaders and volunteers in ministry-specific areas such as: small groups, preaching and teaching, the arts, children, students, volunteers, stewardship, etc.

- **Willow Creek Resources®**—provides churches with trusted and field-tested ministry resources in such areas as leadership, evangelism, spiritual formation, spiritual gifts, small groups, stewardship, student ministry, children's ministry, the use of the arts-drama, media, contemporary music—and more.

- **WCA Member Benefits**—includes substantial discounts to WCA training events, a 20 percent discount on all Willow Creek Resources®, *Defining Moments* monthly audio journal for leaders, quarterly *Willow* magazine, access to a Members-Only section on WillowNet, monthly communications, and more. Member Churches also receive special discounts and premier services through WCA's growing number of ministry partners—Select Service Providers—and save an average of $500 annually depending on the level of engagement.

For specific information about WCA conferences, resources, membership, and other ministry services contact:

Willow Creek Association
P.O. Box 3188, Barrington, IL 60011-3188
Phone: 847-570-9812, Fax: 847-765-5046

www.willowcreek.com

The Unexpected Adventure

Taking Everyday Risks to Talk with People about Jesus

Lee Strobel and Mark Mittelberg

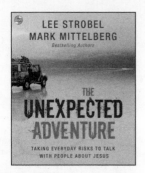

When we seize opportunities to talk with others about Jesus, days that start out dull and tedious can quickly blossom into exciting escapades. Written for today's multigenerational, multicultural world, *The Unexpected Adventure* helps readers take easy steps into a natural evangelistic lifestyle that will energize their own faith while making an eternal difference in the lives of people they encounter.

Using a devotional-style format, bestselling authors Lee Strobel and Mark Mittelberg tell dramatic and sometimes funny stories from their own lives and then draw out practical applications backed by Scripture. Readers will be inspired with fresh compassion for their spiritually confused friends and equipped with practical strategies for influencing others for Christ. Entire churches will be rejuvenated as congregations discover that evangelism can be the adventure of a lifetime — starting today.

Audio CD, Unabridged: 978-0-310-28956-2

Pick up a copy today at your favorite bookstore!

The Case for the Real Jesus

A Journalist Investigates Current Attacks on the Identity of Christ

Lee Strobel
New York Times *Bestselling Author*

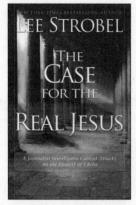

Has modern scholarship debunked the traditional Christ? Has the church suppressed the truth about Jesus to advance its own agenda? What if the real Jesus is far different from the atoning Savior worshipped through the centuries?

In *The Case for the Real Jesus*, former award-winning legal editor Lee Strobel explores such hot-button questions as:

- Did the church suppress ancient non-biblical documents that paint a more accurate picture of Jesus than the four Gospels?
- Did the church distort the truth about Jesus by tampering with early New Testament texts?
- Do new insights and explanations finally disprove the resurrection?
- Have fresh arguments disqualified Jesus from being the Messiah?
- Did Christianity steal its core ideas from earlier mythology?

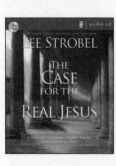

Evaluate the arguments and evidence being advanced by prominent atheists, liberal theologians, Muslim scholars, and others. Sift through expert testimony. Then reach your own verdict in *The Case for the Real Jesus*.

Softcover: 978-0-310-29201-2
Audio CD, Unabridged: 978-0-310-27539-8

Pick up a copy today at your favorite bookstore!

The Case for Christ

A Journalist's Personal
Investigation of the Evidence
for Jesus

Lee Strobel
New York Times *Bestselling Author*

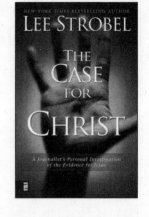

*A Seasoned Journalist Chases Down
the Biggest Story in History*

Is there credible evidence that Jesus of Nazareth really is the Son
of God?

Retracing his own spiritual journey from atheism to faith, Lee Strobel,
former legal editor of the *Chicago Tribune*, cross-examines a dozen
experts with doctorates from schools like Cambridge, Princeton, and
Brandeis who are recognized authorities in their own fields.

Strobel challenges them with questions like How reliable is the
New Testament? Does evidence for Jesus exist outside the Bible? Is
there any reason to believe the resurrection was an actual event?

Strobel's tough, point-blank questions make this Gold Medallion-
winning book read like a captivating, fast-paced novel. But it's not
fiction. It's a riveting quest for the truth about history's most compelling figure.

What will your verdict be in *The Case for Christ*?

*"Lee Strobel probes with bulldog-like tenacity the evidence for the
truth of biblical Christianity."*

Bruce M. Metzger, PhD, Professor of New Testament,
Emeritus, Princeton Theological Seminary

*"Lee Strobel asks the questions a tough-minded skeptic would ask.
His book is so good I read it out loud to my wife evenings after dinner.
Every inquirer should have it."*

Phillip E. Johnson, Law Professor, University of California at Berkeley

Softcover: 978-0-310-20930-0

The Case for Christ — Student Edition

A Journalist's Personal Investigation of the Evidence for Jesus

Lee Strobel with Jane Vogel

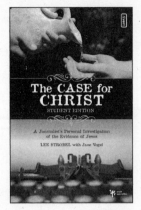

There's little question that he actually lived. But miracles? Rising from the dead? Some of the stories you hear about him sound like just that — stories. A reasonable person would never believe them, let alone the claim that he's the only way to God!

But a reasonable person would also make sure that he or she understood the facts before jumping to conclusions. That's why Lee Strobel — an award-winning legal journalist with a knack for asking tough questions — decided to investigate Jesus for himself. An atheist, Strobel felt certain his findings would bring Christianity's claims about Jesus tumbling down like a house of cards.

He was in for the surprise of his life. Join him as he retraces his journey from skepticism to faith. You'll consult expert testimony as you sift through the truths that history, science, psychiatry, literature, and religion reveal. Like Strobel, you'll be amazed at the evidence — how much there is, how strong it is, and what it says.

The facts are in. What will your verdict be in *The Case for Christ*?

Softcover: 978-0-310-23484-5

Pick up a copy today at your favorite bookstore!

The Case for Christmas

A Journalist Investigates the Identity of the Child in the Manger

Lee Strobel
New York Times *Bestselling Author*

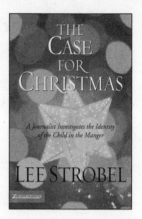

Who was in the manger that first Christmas morning?

Some say he would become a great moral leader. Others, a social critic. Still others view Jesus as a profound philosopher, a rabbi, a feminist, a prophet, and more. Many are convinced he was the divine Son of God.

Who was he — really? And how can you know for sure?

Consulting experts on the Bible, archaeology, and messianic prophecy, Lee Strobel searches out the true identity of the child in the manger. Join him as he asks the tough, pointed questions you'd expect from an award-winning legal journalist. If Jesus really was God in the flesh, then there ought to be credible evidence, including

Eyewitness Evidence — Can the biographies of Jesus be trusted?

Scientific Evidence — What does archaeology reveal?

Profile Evidence — Did Jesus fulfill the attributes of God?

Fingerprint Evidence — Did Jesus uniquely match the identity of the Messiah?

The Case for Christmas invites you to consider why Christmas matters in the first place. Somewhere beyond the traditions of the holiday lies the truth. It may be more compelling than you've realized. Weigh the facts . . . and decide for yourself.

Hardcover, Jacketed: 978-0-310-26629-7

Pick up a copy today at your favorite bookstore!

The Case for a Creator

A Journalist Investigates Scientific Evidence That Points Toward God

Lee Strobel
New York Times *Bestselling Author*

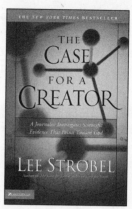

A Journalist Investigates Scientific Evidence That Points Toward God

"My road to atheism was paved by science . . . But, ironically, so was my later journey to God." — Lee Strobel

During his academic years, Lee Strobel became convinced that God was outmoded, a belief that colored his ensuing career as an award-winning journalist at the *Chicago Tribune*. Science had made the idea of a Creator irrelevant — or so Strobel thought.

But today science is pointing in a different direction. In recent years, a diverse and impressive body of research has increasingly supported the conclusion that the universe was intelligently designed. At the same time, Darwinism has faltered in the face of concrete facts and hard reason.

Has science discovered God? At the very least, it's giving faith an immense boost as new findings emerge about the incredible complexity of our universe. Join Strobel as he reexamines the theories that once led him away from God. Through his compelling and highly readable account, you'll encounter the mind-stretching discoveries from cosmology, cellular biology, DNA research, astronomy, physics, and human consciousness that present astonishing evidence in *The Case for a Creator*.

Mass market edition available in packs of six.

Softcover: 978-0-310-24050-1

Pick up a copy today at your favorite bookstore!

The Case for Faith

A Journalist Investigates the Toughest Objections to Christianity

Lee Strobel
New York Times *Bestselling Author*

Was God telling the truth when he said, "You will seek me and find me when you seek me with all your heart"?

In his #1 bestseller *The Case for Christ*, Lee Strobel examined the claims of Christ, reaching the hard-won verdict that Jesus is God's unique son. In *The Case for Faith*, Strobel turns his skills to the most persistent emotional objections to belief—the eight "heart barriers" to faith. This Gold Medallion-winning book is for those who may be feeling attracted to Jesus but who are faced with difficult questions standing squarely in their path. For Christians, it will deepen their convictions and give them fresh confidence in discussing Christianity with even their most skeptical friends.

> *"Everyone—seekers, doubters, fervent believers—benefits when Lee Strobel hits the road in search of answers, as he does again in The Case for Faith. In the course of his probing interviews, some of the toughest intellectual obstacles to faith fall away."*
>
> Luis Palau

> *"Lee Strobel has given believers and skeptics alike a gift in this book. He does not avoid seeking the most difficult questions imaginable, and refuses to provide simplistic answers that do more harm than good."*
>
> **Jerry Sittser**, professor of religion, Whitworth College, and author of *A Grace Disguised* and *The Will of God as a Way of Life*

Softcover: 978-0-310-23469-2

Pick up a copy today at your favorite bookstore!

ZONDERVAN®
.com

The Case for Faith DVD

A Six-Session Investigation of
the Toughest Objections to
Christianity

Lee Strobel and Garry Poole

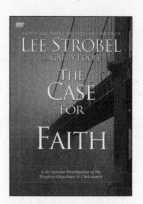

Doubt is familiar territory for Lee Strobel, the
former atheist and award-winning author of
books for skeptics and Christians. But he believes that faith and reason go hand in hand, and that Christianity is a defensible religion.

In this six-session video curriculum, Strobel uses his journalistic
approach to explore the most common emotional obstacles to faith
in Christ. These include the natural inclination to wrestle with faith
and doubt, the troubling presence of evil and suffering in the world,
and the exclusivity of the Christian gospel. They also include this
compelling question: Can I doubt and be a Christian?

Through compelling video of personal stories and experts addressing these topics, combined with reflection and interaction,
Christians and spiritual seekers will learn how to overcome these obstacles, deepen their spiritual convictions, and find new confidence
that Christianity is a reasonable faith.

DVD-ROM: 978-0-310-24116-4

Pick up a copy today at your favorite bookstore!

Becoming a Contagious Church

Increasing Your Church's Evangelistic Temperature

Mark Mittelberg

Evangelism. It's one of the highest values in the church. So why do so few churches put real effort into it? Maybe it's because we don't understand the evangelistic potential of the church well enough to get excited about it. *Becoming a Contagious Church* will change that.

Revised and updated, this streamlined edition dispels outdated preconceptions and reveals evangelism as it really can be. What's more, it walks you through a 6-Stage Process and includes a brand-new 6-Stage Process assessment tool for taking your church beyond mere talk to infections energy, action, and lasting commitment.

> *"This book is not optional! It's required reading for all who are serious about reaching their communities for Christ. Ignoring this book would be pastoral malpractice!"*
>
> **Lee Strobel**, author of *The Case for the Real Jesus*

> *"You can't read this book without having your heart stirred to share the gospel. It's contagious!"*
>
> **Rick Warren**, author of *The Purpose Driven® Church* and *The Purpose Driven® Life*

> *"Entire leadership teams and outreach committees should read and discuss this powerful book — and then put its principles into action."*
>
> **John Maxwell**, author of *Developing Leaders Around You*

> *"I can't emphasize how important books like this one are for the future of the church. It demythologizes the fear and awkwardness of evangelism into something biblical, tangible, and practical for every person."*
>
> **Dan Kimball**, author of *They Like Jesus but Not the Church*

Softcover: 978-0-310-27919-8

Becoming a Contagious Christian

Six Sessions on Communicating Your Faith in a Style That Fits You

Mark Mittelberg, Lee Strobel, and Bill Hybels

Over one million people have experienced the groundbreaking evangelism training course *Becoming a Contagious Christian* — a proven resource designed to equip believers for relational evangelism. Now revised and updated, it avoids stereotyped approaches that feel intimidating to many Christians — and to their friends! Instead, it shows ordinary believers how to share the gospel in natural and effective ways while being the person God made them to be.

Participants experience six 50-minute sessions:
- The Benefits of Becoming a Contagious Christian
- Being Yourself — and Impacting Others
- Deepening Your Relationships and Conversations
- Telling Your Story
- Communicating God's Message
- Helping Your Friends Cross the Line of Faith

DVD Set Includes:
- Forty-page DVD Leader's Guide
- Two 180-minute DVDs
- Complete course teaching by Mark Mittelberg and Lee Strobel
- All-new vignettes, including dramas, interviews, and person-on-the-street segments

DVD: 978-0-310-25788-2

Pick up a copy today at your favorite bookstore!

ZONDERVAN®
.com

Share Your Thoughts

With the Author: Your comments will be forwarded to the author when you send them to *zauthor@zondervan.com*.

With Zondervan: Submit your review of this book by writing to *zreview@zondervan.com*.

Free Online Resources at

www.zondervan.com

Zondervan AuthorTracker: Be notified whenever your favorite authors publish new books, go on tour, or post an update about what's happening in their lives.

Daily Bible Verses and Devotions: Enrich your life with daily Bible verses or devotions that help you start every morning focused on God.

Free Email Publications: Sign up for newsletters on fiction, Christian living, church ministry, parenting, and more.

Zondervan Bible Search: Find and compare Bible passages in a variety of translations at www.zondervanbiblesearch.com.

Other Benefits: Register yourself to receive online benefits like coupons and special offers, or to participate in research.